Ships, Ivory
and Haggis

A journey through change in Britain

Tom Spring

British Library Cataloguing in Publication Data.
A catalogue record for this book is available from the British Library

ISBN 978 086071 722 5

Printed by Moorleys Print & Publishing Ltd

info@moorleys.co.uk / www.moorleys.co.uk

Foreword and Acknowledgements

*W*hat follows is more or less a true account of the events that shaped my life as I remember them and a picture of the times in which I have lived. It is in two parts of which this is the second. This isn't necessarily history as it really was, but as Dr. Johnson said, if a man could say nothing but what he could prove, history couldn't be written. Facts and truth are slippery customers at the best of times, especially when based on personal recollections, and the post-modernists tell us there's no such thing as an objective truth anyway. Besides which, facts – if they exist – ought never to get in the way of a story. If my story has any general interest, and I hope it has, then it lies in the fact that I consider myself to have lived in what history may remember as particularly interesting times.

I began with the idea of providing a simple 'historical' record for our children but a propensity for telling stories and a love of words and phrases hijacked the enterprise and gave it its present form. It became in part a kind of 'thank you' to family and friends who'd had to put up with my 'want of wit' over the years.

Some good friends, Helen first, then John, Mike, Stan, Eric, Gillian and Joe, read and commented on the first draft and offered advice and encouragement. Later I sought professional advice from Hilary Johnson which proved immensely helpful. My wife had to put up with me retiring to my shed for much of three years. She did so with clenched teeth. I'm very grateful to them all, including my wife's dentist.

Tom Spring.

Contents

Ch.1: *Planet Sheffield*

Sheffield! We stepped out into a din of steam engines, traffic, and a myriad of half understood voices calling out. Outside the sky was gun-metal grey and the buildings, in dark red brick or smoke-blackened stone, were mottled. So here I was, hobbling about on crutches, my right leg in a full pot, my brother James in charge of my suitcase, back in my native county only eight days after being discharged from Poplar Hospital. The air was cooler than in London but invigorating, not cold – what you'd expect in the land of forever autumn. I was intoxicated.

We had to find a No.51 bus to take us up to Broomhill and this proved easy enough with the help of the porter who led us across the concourse and pointed out the relevant bus stop. I hadn't been called 'luv' since I was a child! The streets were full of yellow and blue buses jostling with yellow and blue trams but we quickly found ours. On we went, up past Firth Hall – so *this* was a university – and on to Broomhill, which seemed to be where the city started to dissolve into suburbs. We had been given the address of the 'outside rooms' where I was to stay, and informed when lunch was to be served at Robertson Hall, my Hall of Residence. It seemed to make best sense to deposit my stuff at the rooms and head for the Hall for lunch immediately.

No.5 Dawson Road was a very substantial property on three floors. We climbed up the massive stone steps to the biggest front door I'd ever seen. Our first task would be to introduce ourselves and then immediately to leave for lunch. When James rang the bell two elderly ladies appeared: Miss Reeves, a retired primary headmistress and her friend Miss Shaw who worked for a firm of lawyers. He introduced us. Miss Shaw leaned forward and pinched my cheek: 'Bye, you're a bonny lad!' Miss Reeves was a little more restrained but none the less welcoming. We needn't have fretted about our sudden exit. Miss Reeves began with: 'You'll want to drop your stuff off and get down to Robertson for your lunch before they stop serving. We'll be here all afternoon.' We deposited the suitcase in my room – *my* room! As well as the bed there was an ancient gas fire with a much pummelled easy-chair to one side, a writing table and straight-backed Edwardian chair set by a large window that looked out onto the garden, a bookcase, and a substantial oak wardrobe and chest of drawers. A faded Indian carpet covered much of the dark lino. Instructions on how to get to Robertson were given, and off we set down a steep hill as a watery sun began to break through.

Robertson Hall took 180 students but had rooms for only 170, so ten students lived in 'outside rooms'. This meant that they took all their meals in Hall and were included in all Hall activities but they had to sleep nearby. My room was the least nearby and being at the top of the hill, the most difficult to get to: Sod's Law! Robertson was a neo-Georgian building set in substantial and attractive grounds. A porter spotted us as we came through the main entrance, made a note of my name, showed us into a busy dining hall with long tables and explained how we got our meals: sausage and mash with onion gravy, followed by apple crumble and custard.

We'd just started on the crumble when the doors of the dining hall burst open and a group of young women appeared dressed in 'togas', hair held up by large combs: Roman maidens. They were being chased by a raucous mob of males dressed normally.

2

Pandemonium! The maidens exited stage left, at speed. A few minutes later they staggered back dripping wet, breasts and backsides exposed in sharp outline by the wet drapes: they'd been put in the showers. Soon there wasn't a Roman to be seen, only a series of small pools of water. This was Rag Week, though I had no idea what that meant. 'Know what, Jim? I think I'm going to like it here,' I confided. What might those Romans do for me?

Lunch over we made our way back up the hill to Dawson Road. Miss Reeves and Miss Shaw seemed to enjoy having young people around them and were charming. There was one other young gentleman in residence, said Miss Reeves, and he was intending to come and introduce himself and take me down for dinner for 6.30pm. Time now for James to leave, and I didn't find saying goodbye hard. I was dazzled by my new world, and for Jim, well, he would surely report favourably on the events of the day and tell my mum and dad that for a change their younger son had landed on his feet and not on his head.

I went up to my room and started to unpack. Around five thirty there was a knock at the door. Philip Standish appeared, thrust his hand forward confidently: 'You must be Tom; I'm Philip. Welcome to Sheffield,' he said in a proprietorial way. I was impressed. Philip was of average height with wavy, copper hair, a youthful face and a quick smile. He was dressed in the style known – though not to me – as 'smart but causal'. Philip came from the Somerset coast, near Weston. His parents were school teachers and so he was – what, middle-middle class? Moreover we were later to discover that his mother, who hailed originally from Stepney, had gone to the same grammar school as my mother, though they hadn't known each other.

We had no problems getting on and from the beginning Philip didn't wait to be asked to help, and with my physical limitations I often needed help. That saved me some embarrassment. He turned out to be a man of action with a natural capacity for making choices and taking decisions: he didn't do nuance or complexity. Sometime after 6pm we headed down to Robertson. Dinner on Saturday was informal, so we didn't have to wear our gowns. Philip introduced me to a couple of friends, Norman Bentley, known affectionately as Roy, after the Chelsea centre-forward, and Andy Lynch, a rangy Liverpudlian. Roy was the first public school boy I'd ever met. He was to demonstrate a wider vocabulary than I was used to, liberally adorned with expletives, and had a Black Country accent. He was stocky, dressed like a fifty-year old and smoked. Andy by contrast had a loose, athletic frame, and spoke rather quietly with a strong accent, which meant that I had to pay close attention. This odd couple shared a room in Robertson's stylish Victorian annex, known as Birchdale. Both were good company, though not for each other.

After dinner they decided to take me on a brief tour of the charms of Robertson. Roy didn't deign to join us but we agreed to meet him over in Birchdale later when we would all go out to the local pub. The TV room, half-full at the time, only really came to life when sport was televised, which was infrequently and for Discos, known to us as 'Hops'. There was a small bar that opened at the weekend and on special occasions, and a snooker room. These constituted the principal social facilities, though there was one portable gramophone, which you could hire if you had some records. I took my jazz collection up the following term.

Philip, Andy and I walked over to Birchdale, past the tennis court and round the dingle. Roy and Andy shared a study bedroom on the first floor but they had decided to swap so that Andy could share with Robbie from Manchester and Roy would scuttle along the corridor to share with Alasdair Brown, another public school boy. Roy and Robbie were just completing the move as we arrived, and we soon set off for my first visit to the local where, over the next four years, I would become a regular. My first day in Sheffield had been magical. The prospect of living this life for the next few years utterly entranced me. I ended that day as I would many another, in the company of Joshua Tetley of Leeds.

Andy – Lulu as he was affectionately known – had two principal passions: Lesley his hairdresser girlfriend and soccer. According to Andy he and Lesley spent most of their waking hours in coitus, especially during her lunch breaks, at the back of the hairdresser's where she worked. He still found time and energy to be a very skilful and aggressive wing-half (midfielder). He had played representative soccer for Lancashire and would go on to captain the University Firsts and the Robertson Hall team.

Robbie was a dedicated follower of fashion. He held to a view popular down Deansgate that what Manchester wore today the rest of the world would wear tomorrow, and indeed if 'the rest of the world' meant Milnrow, Rawtenstall and Ramsbottom, there may well have been something in this. He had closely-trimmed sideburns and wore rimless glasses. Robbie saw himself as a go-getter and a lady's man. You could swap sentences with Robbie but never really hold a conversation. He knew what he wanted in life and fertilising the soil of social discourse wasn't his prime interest.

Roy was possibly the one man in Robertson who made Robbie look stylish. I found him a revelation; he knew so much. His main passion was serious music and above all English choral music:

Purcell and Tallis, whose music I knew a little of from my days in the school choir and William Byrd, of whom, until then, I'd never even hyrd. Roy introduced me to classical music. In those days the Hallé Orchestra played every week in Sheffield and Manchester over the winter. Roy took me along and told me what to listen for. What's more, he was well read and knowledgeable about British social and political history. And what was he reading at Sheffield? Mechanical Engineering. He said he wanted to be a useful citizen. Trouble was he hated it and was to fail his degree.

As I settled I made more friends, friends I would have for life. Gareth Roberts was a Biologist from Leeds, with an impulsive smile, a sharp, idiosyncratic sense of humour and an old-fashioned moral probity that would often colour his humour with irony. He appeared not to take himself – or indeed anything – seriously; but behind this was a whiff of carbolic soap and hair shirts. Kieran Connor, the product of a posh West London Roman Catholic private school, was a well-spoken and laid-back (he would say) London Irishman with a bit of a Wildean wit. He had a nose for injustice which would fire him throughout his career. On the other hand his social connections gave him a feeling for and a sense of entitlement to the good life. Kieran had a taste for the ridiculous and he and Gareth could bring warmth and laughter to any room and were perfect foils for each other. They were to spend the rest of their lives debating which was the taller. A tough call, though when Gareth began to lose his hair in middle age, Kieran claimed the nudge. Later Gareth got his knees fixed, making his legs less bowed, and he reckoned this made him decisively taller.

Butch Harris, an earnest and decent Brummie Grammar School lad, kind of drifted in and out of the group. He had a wider circle of friends too though he was also something of a loner. He chose to remain on the periphery but was still there fifty years later. When I had hobbled into my first lecture Butch, who didn't know me from a bar of soap, had asked could he help in any way. The last member of our circle was Nathan Samuels, who like Gareth was from Leeds – in fact they had gone to the same school. His father, a tailor, had kitted his only son out elegantly with a mohair suit. Nathan was a man of considerable physical and mental strength, resilience and integrity but underneath these virtues a sense of vulnerability would occasionally peek out. Nathan had been brought up as a good Jewish boy. He had never consumed alcohol, except in small quantities for religious purposes, and never been with a woman. Perhaps he thought by attaching himself to us these deficiencies might be rectified. We would be happy to do our best.

We were a socially diverse lot in Robertson though the great majority was middle-class. I was kind of used to being in a minority since most of my fellow sixth-formers had been middle-class. Philip once enumerated the wide range of expertise that the fathers of our circle could provide, which might benefit any of us in our future careers; he concluded with the observation that if anyone should find themselves in need of a barge, my dad was the go-to man. One evening only a week after I arrived, a group of Robertsonians were having a drink in town and someone started singing their regional songs. We had *She's a Lassie from Lancashire*, *The Blaydon Races*, *Maggie May*, *Maybe it's because I'm a Londoner* – all well received, even *Ilkley Moor*. Then a sandy haired toff with a pock-marked face sang *The Eton Boating Song*, rather well actually, and someone emptied a pint over him. Unforgivable: it was Younger's No.3.

7

In the first year of an Honours course Sheffield students were required to study four subjects, including their intended Honours subject – History for me. However, if you had acquired an 'A' at A Level you were permitted to drop one subject though not your Honours subject, so I decided to drop French. Had there been anyone to advise me I would have dropped German too and opted for a new subject, like Philosophy say, but there wasn't. I was very happy to continue with English for my third subject. As for History, having arrived three weeks late, I found myself having to write an essay after only a week on why the Renaissance had occurred in Italy when it did. My supervisor was of the opinion that if I were given a time extension it would only clutter up my later writing commitments. I didn't know much about the Renaissance and even less about contemporary Italy, but with Roy's promptings I managed.

Wearing a pot got me noticed and earned me some sympathy. For example, it prompted the appearance of a pale green envelope in my pigeon hole containing a card with a hand-written invitation: 'Mr. Ricky Fotheringham requests the company of Mr. Thomas Spring for pre-prandial drinks in his room in Birchdale at 17.30 on Thursday of next week.' So: plenty of time to find out what pre-prandial meant. For me this invitation might have come from another planet. Dinner at Robertson was formal, which meant we wore, amongst other things, a white shirt, a tie and an academic gown, and the six who assembled at Ricky's on the appointed hour that Thursday were suitably attired. Four, including the host, sported bow ties. I was one of two eighteen-year olds, the other four were ex-servicemen maybe ten years older. It was a bizarre experience though by no means an unpleasant one, but I was relieved that, being in outside rooms, I wouldn't be expected to reciprocate.

I had been up at Sheffield for a couple of weeks when I got a letter from Red McCain, one of the nurses who had brightened up my stay in hospital, answering one I'd written to her. Mine had been a 'thank you' letter, kind of hoping that we might meet when I was home at Christmas. Hers was a 'you're welcome' letter, kind of insisting that we wouldn't. She added a post-script that made my heart stop: fancy your father finishing up in the same bed in the same ward as yourself! *W-h-a-t?* Phone calls home in those days were rare but one was definitely needed here, and it was made immediately, and with the greatest trepidation. It seemed that my dad had been helping in the unloading of timber from the hold of a Swedish cargo ship when a plank had sprung outwards and cuffed his forehead, fracturing his skull. Since it had been a glancing blow the damage wasn't horrendous but he finished up in his son's hospital bed for a week and was off work for more than a month. When finally he got back to work it was to discover that his compensation would be minimal because he shouldn't have been in the hold at all. The fact that he had been breaking this rule to get the job done was, so the owners said, given due consideration when compensation was calculated. £1,200 wasn't much: better to stick your finger into a machine like my friend Arthur. The family had considered it best not to worry me, what with all I had on my plate. My mum came to believe that her man was permanently affected by this accident, becoming shorter tempered, and who would know better than she? Ten days later a letter came from my mum with even more bad news: James had made it a hat trick for the Springs! It seems he had been weight-training in the local gym when he overdid things and gave himself a fearsome swelling requiring an immediate operation. He, too, spent a week at the mercy of Red and her friends in that very same bed. You'd have thought we Springs would have been awarded the bed to keep. And maybe Red too.

Meanwhile I'd been transferred from Poplar Hospital to the Royal Hallamshire in Sheffield where, in early November the doctors took off my original plaster but disappointingly decided to replace it. The sight of my naked leg after over three months' incarceration horrified me. It was an inch shorter now and at the break there was an ugly knuckle of bone that would diminish but never disappear. My leg was painfully thin and caked with dried blood. As it was scraped off, the lint took skin and hair with it, leaving globules of blood everywhere. The doctors decided that this was a good time to swap my crutches for a walking stick, reducing me at a stroke from power walking to a pathetic shuffle. I was very low and mostly stayed in my room for the rest of that week, dragging myself out only to eat meals. Philip suggested that to take my mind off my condition I might write a draft of his English essay. Well, I owed him that at least.

My poorly leg wouldn't see the light of day again until the following January when I finally lost my pot. I asked how long before I could play football but the medical profession was non-committal. Lucky to be able to walk said one; the path to fitness would prove long and very rocky, said another. When later that academic year I felt able, I tried to run but was never free from pain. In the following year I would play several games of soccer for the University Third Eleven, but I suffered agonies over the following days. I decided to give it up. After my last game, as we traipsed off, I was approached by a middle-aged man in a duffel coat who asked my age. 'Oh, right,' he said, 'only if you'd been younger we might've been interested in you.' I explained why they wouldn't, but who were the 'we'? 'Wednesday, lad, I'm t'physio.' I explained my condition and he shook his head. He'd spent half a life-time dealing with this kind of injury, he said, and could certainly help me. 'It'll cost, mind and I doubt tha'll ever play for England.' I trusted this man and my parents undertook to fund the programme – the equivalent of about £500 – and ten weeks of electrical treatment and physiotherapy and a specialised exercise regime followed which put an end to my agonies. He was as good as his word; I never did play for England. My chief sporting assets, speed and strength, had been permanently compromised; I'd never really be much good, whatever I played. All the same he gave me a lifetime of pleasure from sport, starting with university rugby.

All this lay ahead of me: in that first term playing sport formed no part of my life. But there was so much else. Those in Robertson who had done military service had seen a lot of the world. They were older, wiser and more articulate, and would often be part of our group discussions which covered politics, the arts, and life-in-general into the small hours. I soon realised how uncultivated I was and began to take steps to put this right – and without sport I had the time. This 'education' was far more lively and enriching than my academic tuition: it blew my mind. When I returned to London at the end of that magical first term, though I might still be wearing a pot and walk with a stick I was truly a changed man. I even spoke differently. My family would have noticed the change; I hope they didn't mind.

Christmas was better than ever. My dad and Jimmy looked their normal selves but my mum seemed older, wearier. I realised how much I'd missed them and New Year celebrations took on a deeper significance for me. As always the house filled with my aunts, uncles and cousins and there was the customary dancing and singing. Just before midnight everybody trooped out into the street, with cooking pots. When at midnight the hooters of all the ships in the docks engulfed the whole island we bashed our pots to welcome in the New Year, joined hands for *Auld Lang Syne* and finished with our anthem, the *Miner's Lament*, about a miner, far from home, who dreams of England's valleys and dells, and the village bells ringing in the New Year. I've never met another soul who knew it. After my dad's death about a quarter of a century later we stopped singing it and a chunk of me died with it. I still sing it to myself quietly: it conjures up the thrum of the docks, the bustle of factories, the hooters at New Year, the banter, the songs, the sense of tribal community, the poverty, the violence, the noise, the drabness and the limited horizons.

Much as I rejoiced in this tribal reaffirmation of my roots I think I knew then that I would never return to the Island. I had grown up and though I had no idea what I would do with my life I did know that I wouldn't be doing it here. In only seven weeks Sheffield had changed me, opening the door on an unimagined world. I needed to go through that door. Ahead was the unknown and surely, as Joe Gargery might have said: such larks!

Ch.2: *A Life of Reilly*

For those unencumbered by broken limbs life in a men's Hall of Residence in those days revolved around sport, women and mateship. The consumption of alcohol was intimately involved in each but hardly constituted an independent category: unlike today's students we rarely went out just to get rat-arsed. Social events like Rag Week featured strongly in the calendar. Almost non-existent in university life today, Rag Week encouraged students to do crazy things, ostensibly to raise money for charities. The sudden arrival of those Roman maidens on my first visit to Robertson had been associated with a Rag event. Once we pulled a jangling piano nearly fifty miles from Sheffield to Nottingham. It rained; before we'd even managed the first long hill out of Sheffield all the keys had jammed and we ceased to jangle. On we trudged regardless, in shifts, through continuous rain, taking breaks for hot tea from our back-up van. We hit Nottingham during the morning rush hour, in sunshine, and managed to raise quite a bit of cash from startled commuters. A regular feature of Rag Week was a tug-o'-war with our rival Hall for a barrel of Ward's ale. The *Barrel Pull*, involving 180 per side, was held every year for a quarter of a century and Robertson managed to lose every year.

Robertson Hall had strict rules concerning female guests: no women could be entertained after 6pm during the week and after 10.30pm at the weekend. In those days to indulge in sex before marriage was not only fraught with practical difficulties but stood against social custom, religious dogma, moral convention and parental approval. All the Halls at Sheffield were single sex. The Warden and his colleagues on High Table stood *in loco parentis* for all students under the age of 21, but realistically all they could do was make things difficult for would-be miscreants. Once, in my second year, I was escorting a young lady off the premises just after midnight when, in the distance, I saw the Warden doing his rounds and immediately went to ground: I didn't think he'd seen me. Several days later, however, he stopped me after dinner and asked what I had been doing that night. I explained that I was going down for a game of squash, something which was often done at any time of day or night especially when we were working on a project. 'I see. And does your opponent always were high heels?' he enquired archly. Next time I would be out on my ear. Ours was the last generation for whom sex was licensed – and scarce. I'm convinced Dostoevsky got it right: if everything is permitted, where's the fun in anything?

Though having a leg in plaster in that first term had opened unexpected doors, none gave onto romance: I had been chaste. In the new term, with my leg recently liberated, I could go to a Hop! The Saturday in January after my plaster came off I found myself dancing with a willowy dark-haired nurse called Jenny, whose friend Liz had been draped around Robbie's neck for much of the evening. They had to leave shortly after ten but Robbie had arranged to meet Liz the following Saturday. Now Liz went nowhere without her friend Jenny so Robbie had kindly committed me to take care of Jenny. OK by me.

Here was the plan: we were to meet for a drink and then repair to Robbie's room: room-mate Andy would be away in Liverpool. We would play some music on the Hall gramophone; have a

14

smooch and then, who knows? But just in case he got lucky, Robbie had the use of Alasdair and Roy's room nearby for the evening. The following Saturday we met, had a drink – in Liz's case several drinks – and then came back to Birchdale. We listened to music, we smooched, and then Robbie and Liz sloped off to Alasdair's. As Jenny and I were becoming better acquainted, the door burst open, the light flashed on and a dishevelled Liz charged in. 'Come on Jenny, we're going home,' she exploded. 'That...that... *man* has only been trying to *screw* me.' Jenny, adjusting her blouse, put her arm round Liz and escorted her out of the room to calm her down, looking back apologetically over her shoulder and mouthing: 'I'll be back directly luv.'

Robbie meanwhile had phoned another nurse unaware that Liz and Jenny had been in earshot and when they came back Liz was incandescent. 'The bastard's only arranging to screw someone else now. We'll see about that!' 'Come on Liz luv, let's get you back to the hostel,' Jenny coaxed, but Liz's fury brought a flash of inspiration: 'Wardrobe!' she exclaimed, yanking open the door and tumbling in. Just then Robbie reappeared and began to list his grievances against the Yorkshire nursing sorority in general and one of its members in particular. He was cut short in mid-tirade by an advancing wardrobe. He stood riveted to the spot, his jaw dropped, his eyes bulged. 'Jesus, Mary and bloody Joseph!' he yelped and fled the room. Ayckbourn could have written that scene; such larks!

Towards the end of the term we organised a party to launch Nathan Samuels on the life of sensual pleasures for which he had been itching. We would invite women from a local nurses' hostel or teacher-training college, or both, for our occasional parties in Birchdale. On the Saturday in question we invested in crisps, peanuts and sherry, took up the carpets, moved the furniture, draped pink crêpe paper around the lights, put some music on and awaited the arrival of the women. Kieran was the first to offer Nathan a tumbler of sherry, which he sank in no time. No nurses yet. Seeing him clasping an empty tumbler I offered Nathan another. Sound of nurses arriving downstairs: I went to usher them up and so didn't see Nathan dispatch tumbler number two. Philip meanwhile, having returned with his girlfriend, noticed Nathan sitting with an empty tumbler and poured him a refill. In all, he'd put back the equivalent of eight or nine normal-sized sherries. He sat expectantly, eyes twinkling, beaming. I introduced him to Shirley a chatty brunette. Ever the gentleman Nathan got to his feet, still beaming, and put his hand politely out to greet Shirley. However, his trajectory continued through the vertical, past an astonished Shirley and her outstretched hand and down again, knees buckling, onto the floor beyond. Backside in the air he turned his head as if to apologise, but nothing came out. Philip and I set him up in a bath with blankets and pillows. He looked like a corpse, except for that beam. Such larks!

Social life in Robertson was dominated by termly Balls. These were special occasions one of whose highlights was a cabaret. One in particular stays in my mind: because of the part played by one Birchdale resident, Roy Bentley's room-mate Alasdair Brown. Alasdair lived on another planet and was a frequent target for his more worldly friends. Late one evening when we were having coffee he joined us, fresh from amateur dramatics. He had encountered the recently discovered art of method acting which, he explained, was all about actually *becoming* the character you were playing. Alasdair was asked could he envisage 'becoming' hateful characters, say, Hitler. Anybody, said Alasdair. Or an ape-man? Anybody, said Alasdair. How about an inanimate object? He didn't see why not: yes, he felt sure it could be done. Well, could he play, say, a banana? Before our eyes Alasdair Brown *became* a banana. Accounts of his remarkable thespian skill circulated and the Robertson public demanded that he perform in the cabaret at the next Hall Ball.

Talented student and staff entertainers abounded and would provide excellent entertainment. At the Ball in question, for example, a Thai student produced some amazing magic, including removing a girl's bra without her knowing. Then Alasdair made his debut. Now he may not have been the first to portray the humble banana on stage: Josephine Baker's banana dance at the *Folies Bergère* in the 1930s sounded more athletic and possibly more erotic than Alasdair's. When it came to capturing the essence of banana-ness, however, Alasdair definitely had the nudge. Nobody who saw him that night would doubt it. Or forget it. Such larks!

One evening some twenty years later, I was watching a late-night programme on the dangers of nuclear contamination. The Sellafield nuclear plant, known at the time as Windscale, endured a major fire in 1957, so the government, deciding that nothing so bad should ever happen again, instituted a major safety review. The expert on nuclear contamination who was nominated to reassure the public on TV that evening was one Alasdair Brown: *HELP!!* Did his employers know that this saviour of the nation was actually a large piece of fruit?

The three men's halls participated in annual soccer, rugby, hockey and tennis competitions. The soccer and rugby games would draw crowds of maybe a hundred and were contested ferociously. When I had completed my rehabilitation programme at Wednesday I decided to give rugby a try. I played a handful of games, at wing forward, and was beginning to get the hang of it. I was amazed to discover a sport in which knocking people over was regarded as a key skill. What I liked was that each player had a specific role to perform. The forwards made the ball available, the halves created the openings and the backs scored the tries: none of this 'total rugby' nonsense. My job was to try to knock people over and generally win the ball in 'contact situations': it helped that I still had only a flimsy hold on the rules. One Sunday there was to be a trial for the Hall rugby team and I was to play. A few of us had gone off to London for the weekend and driving back up on Sunday we went straight to the ground for the game. It was snowing lightly. My girlfriend, no great aficionado of rugby, or indeed any sport, having come to London, was obliged to watch the game. On this Sunday, for the one and only time in my rugby playing career, I scored two tries. After the game I casually asked what she had thought of the game. 'Not bad,' she replied. *Not bad*? 'So did you like my tries then?' I probed. 'Oh, did you score a try?' she asked incredulously. 'No, actually I scored two bloody tries, but you seem to have missed both.' This is what a cat must feel like when the disembowelled rabbit it presents to its owner at breakfast time is rejected disdainfully. 'Oh, *sorry* Tom. It was so cold out there that I came into the bar to watch from inside.' Frailty, we know where you live! Well, fortunately somebody must have seen because I subsequently made the team.

Although very few students in those days worked during term time most of us took jobs over the summer, to raise cash for the next academic year and to finance holidays. At the end of my first year I took a labourer's job at Charrington's Brewery in the Mile End Road, and spent two months there. I shared my first task of the day with a lean man in his early sixties who was reputed to consume over thirty pints a day – hence the smile. I never kept a tally but could vouch for the fact that he would have consumed eight half-pint cans of IPA by breakfast each day. I enjoyed my stay but never managed to perfect the magical skill of directing upright empty barrels in any trajectory with the flick of a wrist. Some men could curve them round corners.

My second summer was spent working on the roads in Sheffield. After my first morning one of my workmates took me down to the hut for lunch. 'Na then, lad, when tha' goes through t'door tha'll have to mek a massive, *massive* decision: be sure an' get it *reight!*' Conspiratorial wink. When opened, the door revealed a long trestle table with one or two places on the benches on both sides still vacant. On the left side all the mugs were red and white for United and on the right side they were all blue and white for Wednesday. Everyone looked at me expectantly. There was no choice: I owed the blue-and-whites. Cheers and howls in equal measure! I felt more at home with these men than I had with those at the brewery. Though pleasant enough, they had seemed a little suspicious: as though they thought that someone at university, someone 'educated' must be 'better' than they, or anyway think they were better. Paradoxically they also believed that the world of education wasn't the real world and so the educated person was somehow 'less' than they were. Working on the roads in Sheffield, on the other hand, I was aware of no such ambivalence. Rich or poor, educated or not, town or country, we were all the same, though some were red-and-white and others blue-and-white.

Jud, in his thirties, with a thick mop of unruly dark hair and brown eyes that never stayed still, had a very simple attitude to life: always be a little in debt. This was important when we were paid on a Friday instead of a Thursday. Then he would always borrow of a Thursday – though never from me – and always made sure he had a good night. One Friday morning while we were smashing up kerbstones Jud told me he'd borrowed £10 from his dad the night before. 'How come?' I asked, 'we got paid yesterday.' 'Ay, I kno',' he replied, 'but s'poasin' Ah were to get run ovver on t'way hoam, an' I were to snuff it and never owed no booger owt. What good's that?'

My summer jobs helped financed my next year of study, but I also earned enough for a holiday. These holidays, which normally involved hitch-hiking on the continent, were adventures. The first was the most notable; it came at the end of our second year when five of us decided to hitch-hike to the South of France, to a campsite close to the holiday camp where I'd stayed a few years before. The plan was to take a student flight to Paris and spend a few days there before heading south. Paris was a revelation but at the end of our second day, sitting in a bar, we drew lots for our departure the following morning. I was to go at 10am along with Andy. He would stand 100 yards or so beyond me and if I got a lift I was to do my best to wangle a place for him. I had a secret weapon: a large Union Jack sewn to the top of my rucksack, which I would unfurl when in position. Brit or Anglophile drivers might take pity!

Within ten minutes a Mercedes pulled up and a middle-aged man addressed me in German: where was I going, and so on. My German wasn't bad; after all, I'd been studying the subject only the year before. I mentioned my friend down the road – could he be picked up? No problem, and soon Andy's rucksack joined mine in the boot. Andy mentioned that he had seen no sign of the others and assumed they had got off O.K. At this the driver's head swivelled round: 'Sind Sie – *Engländern*?'

All the same, not only did he treat us to lunch, the first time either of us had tried frogs' legs, but he stopped overnight in Lyon and picked us up from the campsite the following morning.

Soon we'd all made it and were enduring the customary accompaniments of a continental holiday – sunburn and the dreaded squitts. We didn't all suffer equally. Nathan and I were less prone to sunburn but Andy was a martyr to it: he was kippered. None of us could afford to be too far from the toilet block. Soon though we were able to put a shirt on without suffering agonies and break wind with scarcely a qualm. Then our days blossomed; we swam, sunbathed, played footie and read, had a few beers at the beach bar: paradise. One day I unaccountably left all my money on the beach and had it stolen. Kieran had the inspiration to organise a party to 'celebrate' and everybody gave me a sub, so I finished up with more money than anyone. Then we all got stonkered. In our second week we encountered a group of women from the metropolis of Glossop. I found myself specially drawn to a well-constructed blonde called Cathy. She danced sinuously, sang raucously, tackled fiercely at footie and when I caressed her breasts her whole body seemed to explode. These were the days of *The Twist*, the only dance that I could say

I'd mastered since Victor Sylvester days. Cathy and I twisted the nights away. Bliss it was to be alive.

Kieran and I stayed on after the others had left, but we were less successful now in chatting up the English girls and to give ourselves a chance we decided to pass ourselves off as Danish. I had become a Viking after all, and a comrade to history's smallest Viking! Being Danish all day proved more difficult than we had imagined – how an earth do the Danes manage? – and our only success came with a pair of secretaries from Manchester. When we first met on the beach one had whispered to her friend that she had the runs. I took her hand in mine: 'you like to run,' I said looking into her eyes, 'I too. In fact I am running for my country Denmark. Perhaps you too are running for Manchester?' Her friend was in convulsions but the girl kept an almost straight face: 'Know what, chuck, these last few days I reckon I have been bloody running for Manchester an' all.'

A few days later we left for home. I decided to head for Chartres rather than Paris, to see the Cathedral, and the colours of that magnificent window in the autumn sun repaid the effort. Back on the open road in my customary position beyond the junction, I unfurled my Union Jack. Shortly after, a French *auto-stoppeur* turned up and stood ten yards in front of me. Mais ce n'est pas le cricket! Then he proceeded to unbutton his trousers, take out his todger and pee: was this a new tactic? A car came round the junction, went straight past him and pulled up just beyond me: it was a Roller. I didn't connect the arrival of this splendid beast with myself. A rotund, balding gentleman got out: 'I say, weren't you looking for a lift?' In a daze I thanked him and made my way over. He turned out to be a Labour Peer of the Realm, on holiday with his wife. They took me on for several hours – it was like riding on a magic carpet – and dropped me where they left the road. I thanked them, stood at the roadside and once more unfurled the colours.

I could see for miles. Nothing! Half an hour later a dot appeared on the horizon. In the slow passage of time it turned into a car. Was it British? Eventually I could identify it as a Renault. Bugger, French number plates. It *had* to stop: there was absolutely nothing behind it all the way to the horizon. But no, it sped past. Then, suddenly: screech of brakes, audible clunk of gears and miraculously the car reversed towards me at speed, pulling up at my side. A middle-aged woman looked out. 'Vous êtes Anglais, monsieur?' They took me on to Calais and insisted that I stay the night with them. Next day, before catching the ferry home, I took the opportunity to go to the square to see Rodin's depiction of those Calais burghers and in the warm drizzle I reflected more fondly than you might think on my primary schooling, on Mr. Stanger and even on his awesome Pimple.

Our other holidays were more ordinary. The following year we hitched down to Spain in pairs, three us of this time with our girlfriends. On our return journey my girlfriend (whom I later married) and I and Kieran and his lady took the train to Avignon, planning to hitch from there. Arriving in the wee small hours of Sunday, we eventually found a flat area down by the river to camp. Tent erected, we zonked out immediately. The sound of voices woke us next morning: we were in the middle of a boules competition. At a nearby bar for coffee and croissants, we saw our tent on TV – it was the regional championships. That tent came down quicker than you could whistle *Sous le Pont* and off we set.

My undergraduate years could hardly have been fuller or more enjoyable. It might seem I left little time for the serious things of life, such as pursuing the scholarly studies for which I had supposedly come to Sheffield, but you'd be well wrong. Sport, women and mateship helped to shape me. I wouldn't underestimate their importance in my education. And such larks…

Ch.3: *Hearts and Minds*

Jo from Battersea elbowed her way into my life towards the end of my second term in Robertson. She was a friend of a theology student I knew. We spoke only briefly when we first met so I was taken aback when mutual friends said that later she would talk of no-one else but me. But wasn't she Stuart's girlfriend? Nevertheless whenever we met later I became aware that her eyes tended to follow me. This had never happened to me before and I was flattered, and began to notice that she was actually very attractive. I spoke to Stuart about her: they weren't an item after all; she had a boyfriend back home. We seemed to keep bumping into each other.

A month or so later, on the last Sunday of the Term, a group of us had taken the coach up to watch an inter-hall rugby match – I was still a non-combatant - with Jo sitting next to Stuart. The two became detached and on the way back she chose the seat next to me. We chatted inconsequentially when, after a while, she said pointedly that she felt cold. I put an arm around her and she snuggled closer. Then, at what seemed the appropriate time I kissed her very discreetly and she responded with unmistakable warmth. 'You can't know how much I've longed for that,' she whispered. I had never been spoken to with such evident – what? We met that evening in the Larkhill Tavern and more or less agreed to become an item. Next day I explained to Stuart that this was no dalliance: he should know that I really felt I had met my soulmate. When I went back to London for the Easter holidays, I had convinced myself that I was in love.

On our return to Sheffield in April Jo and I fixed our attention on the examinations looming at the end of that academic year. To obtain entry into an Honours Class in year two you had to gain 60% in your Honours subject – History for me – and to pass your other subjects – English and German for me. History would be a piece of cake for me since I'd covered pretty much half of the syllabus at A Level – twice. As for English I'd read a lot and felt confident, though I sorely missed the inspiration of George Whitlam. German was as problematical as ever but I hoped that my 'feel' for the literature would pull me through as it had at A Level. Jo was following a course designed specifically for teachers and needed to pass each of her four subjects.

The results came out in the last week of the summer term. I'd easily cleared the History hurdle and had passed English and German. To my dismay however my tutor told me that entry to Honours was in the balance. It seems that I'd only managed a bare pass in both German and English. I wondered whether my English result might be checked, since I'd felt it to be my best paper, and added that I wouldn't return to do a General Degree. That, I thought, would be tantamount to breaking the contract I'd made with my parents.

Before the week was out I got a letter from the Department admitting me to Honours. Two weeks after returning to London for the summer, I received a hand-written letter from the Head of English, the poet William Empson, telling me that although he and his colleagues had thoroughly enjoyed reading my paper, the standard of spelling was appalling and I should not even consider studying the subject to a higher level. What had my old chess opponent said? Bloody sharp if I wasn't such an idiot?

My results may have left something to be desired; Jo's were disastrous. She had to resit all four exams in September. There was no way, she said, that she could continue with her degree. Nonsense, I countered, we would have to institute a regime over the summer so that she could handle the resits successfully. We spent many evenings and weekends together that summer and over the months we melted into each other. By autumn Jo was confident of success and I was very much in love. My family, who had met Jo, had fallen for her too. I saw my soulmate off at King's Cross, confident that she would succeed in her resits.

I left on the first Saturday of October contemplating how different this autumn would be compared to the last. Philip and I now had rooms in Hall and so it was easy to meet up with friends in Robertson, several of whom had been up for a few days. Like Jo, Philip had had to resit his exams and had been up for two weeks. When we met the group seemed strangely subdued and when I said I was going off to meet Jo, mysterious glances were exchanged. 'Tom, mate,' this was Philip, 'there's something you ought to know. No easy way to say this and you won't like it, but your Jo's been seeing quite a lot of Mark Queen.' Pause, another exchange of glances. 'And by quite a lot I mean a lot more than she should've. You've got a problem.' I felt as if I'd been punched in the solar plexus. My head spun, I wanted to vomit. I needed air, needed to cry out. Utterly, utterly distraught I looked at each of them but nobody looked back. I forced myself to say something about sorting it all out and rushed out, in serious danger of detonating.

When I had steeled myself to make that phone call Jo said she had something important to tell me, too important for the 'phone.

We agreed to meet for a coffee. Jo told me then that Mark, captain of the University rugby team, who was also up in Sheffield early, had kept pressing her for a date and finally she had agreed. They got on very well immediately, she said, and now, well, she was no longer sure about anything. I told her that I'd been certain we would be spending the rest of our lives together and that she'd felt the same. How could she possibly even think of... I tailed off. She felt desperately sad and confused, she said, but more than anything she really didn't want to lose me and would always love me, but as a very dear friend. Dagger words! Struggling with a feeling of emptiness that was painful, I managed somehow to mumble that I was her lover or nothing. Silently, plaintively almost, Jo opted for nothing.

Given the choice between a repeat of the previous summer's road accident and its dire consequences and this autumn's break-up, I would have taken the former without hesitation. Unlike those weeks in hospital I had no faith now that things would get better. I had been brought up to believe that there was one woman, tailor-made, for me in this world; all I had to do was find her. Well, I'd found her: or to be more accurate, she'd found me. Tolstoy's Karenin, devastated by the double treachery of his Anna, had cried out wretchedly: what did I ever do to deserve this? It came to me like a hammer blow: this was exactly what I had done to Maria the year before. My pain was no worse than hers, Jo's treachery certainly no worse than mine. I could hardly bear to think of it in these terms but I really *did* deserve all this.

I staggered along from one day to the next. Sleep was hard to come by, my academic studies lost their flavour; I ate little and found no consolation in drink so I didn't. The only way I could lose myself, and that was the summit of my hopes, was by training and lifting weights in the gym and I took to that in a very big way. Agonisingly slowly, things began to get less painful; I spent much of the rest of that term chasing – and sometimes catching – Jo look-alikes. I was Richard III, desperately scouring the field of Bosworth for the real Henry Tudor but finding and killing only his doubles. That I survived the term was due in large part to the support I got from my friends in Robertson. Term finally crept in its petty pace to an end: now for the dreary prospect of a vacation at home without Jo.

Actually things turned out to be far from anti-climactic. Since the early summer James had been going out with a pert, attractive woman from New Cross called Nicky, and they were becoming serious. Shortly before Christmas it became clear how serious: Nicky was three months gone. James and Nicky were in love but neither would have chosen marriage just at that time. On a bitterly cold Saturday in December in the very church where James and I had been choirboys, the young lovers became one. This was the first wedding when I didn't get half-a-crown for singing.

The rest of that second year sped by. I continued to read widely but spent much of the time in the gym. Then early in summer term Kieran and I found ourselves looking at a departmental notice board where a list of our names appeared – all the History and Politics people. It comprised two groups, one small and one quite large and had one single name at the bottom. My name and Kieran's were down the bottom end of the second, larger group. 'What d'you think this is all about K?' I asked. Kieran scrutinised the list. 'Looks like they've listed us according to the class of degrees they think we'll get. Those four at the top will get 2is and the rest of us 2iis, except for Joanie Carver: they've got her down for a 3rd. We're near the bottom of the 2iis, mate.' 'Hang on. What d'you mean, *class* of degrees?' I asked, totally bemused, 'and what the Hell's a 2ii?' 'Well, they obviously don't think too much of us, because we're near the bottom of the 2iis, right?' I grabbed Kieran by the lapels in a frenzy: 'No – *not* right. I don't understand. What's a bloody 2ii?' 'Don't be obtuse,' Kieran muttered, freeing himself with some difficulty, 'degrees are classified, OK? The best are Firsts, but nobody gets those here. Then a few get 2is. Most people get 2iis and some might get 3rds. That's the way it's done, right?' I was stupefied. 'But... I thought we all just got BAs, so long as we played the game. Why didn't you bloody *tell* me?' 'Come on Tom; everybody knows this. Anyway, what's wrong with a 2ii? Most people get one.' 'But the Department hasn't explained any of this stuff, have they? Here we are, halfway through the bloody course, having a great time, and actually we're messing up. Shit! Shit! *Shit!!*' I kicked the skirting board, 'it's not bloody *fair!*' and then I stomped off.

I stole back later. Nobody was about. I studied the names of the putative 2is. At the top was an ex-army man, Malcolm Reece, a smart guy and a hard worker, but no Aristotle. 'Whatever degree you get, sunshine, I'm gonna get the same,' I said, stabbing at Reece's name on the board with my forefinger. I felt just as I had at school when the Fish had predicted that I would get only two O Levels. As Kieran said, nothing wrong with a 2ii but I hadn't come here to get one. I owed my mum and dad more than that. So I buckled down, spending less time in the gym and more in the library and sure enough my written work began to get 'Bs' and 'B+'s instead of 'C's and 'C+'s. Even better I discovered an enthusiasm for studying political thought and managed to impress one of my tutors, a man who looked like one of the beast people in Wells's *Island of Dr. Moreau*: pasty-faced and heavy jowelled with lank black hair and large doleful brown eyes. His interest in my progress gave me a lot of confidence.

Not long into my third year, I began to notice a woman. I'd seen her in the Hall bar towards the end of the previous term and had been struck by a refined face with high cheekbones and green eyes peering out from under the usual bouffant of blond hair. I decided to ask her out. One afternoon, Kieran, Nathan, Butch and I were sharing a table in the library when Miss Oliver sat at a table nearby. 'There she is! So go on then,' said Kieran, 'ask her out for coffee.' 'But she's only just arrived,' I replied defensively. 'Bet you won't, though!' Nathan chipped in and clucked like a chicken. Disapproving glances and coughs from nearby tables! I screwed up my courage, went and whispered 'I know you've only just arrived, but I was planning to go for a coffee in half an hour or so and wondered if you'd like to join me?' Only a slight hesitation then, with a smile: 'That would be nice.' I returned to the table. 'Turned you down eh? Can't say I blame her,' said Nathan. 'Don't bank on it sunshine,' I replied with a smirk. 'Shshsh!!' said nearby tables. Half an hour later I got up to leave, and, to the evident surprise of the comrades, so did my new friend.

Maureen Oliver turned out to be as agreeable as she looked. If not love at first sight I nevertheless felt an immediate and powerful sense of attraction. From the first she saw me as redeemable: her project was to 'civilise' me, make me more acceptably middle class. Some hopes! She herself was a social smoker and a *Daily Telegraph* reader ('only for the crossword' she lied) and *I* set about converting *her* to become one of us. Was my project any more successful? Reader, I married her! Before long Maureen became Mo and I felt comfortable enough to take her home. My mum and dad were very impressed: they thought her quite posh. In fact one of my cousins said that she was the poshest person she'd ever met. Mo spoke correctly and without a Cockney accent, and in the East End that's pretty darned posh. My parents were confident she must come from a moneyed family. Perhaps Mo's father rode to hounds? And all because she didn't say 'I ain't' and 'we wasn't'.

Over the Christmas holidays Mo came down again and stayed for four days, which incorporated the Spring's New Year party. This was a kind of make-or-break for our relationship, since she would meet the tribe out to enjoy itself: ordeal by *Danny Boy*. She went back home to Lincolnshire having suitably impressed the tribe and more importantly having enjoyed herself. Less than a week later we were both back in Sheffield for the new term, at the end of which we had scheduled the return fixture: I would spend a few days with the Olivers in darkest Lincolnshire.

South of the Wolds Lincolnshire stretches to the far horizon without as much as a crease, like some massive billiard table. The inhabitants of the Baltic states think that their lands are flat. Balts, forget it: only the Dutch can compete. Here the skies are immense. Lincolnshire people do not wear their hearts on their sleeves, but if you scratch them you'll find an enduring love of the land in their blood. Once I travelled down to Nottingham by coach to play rugby and found myself sitting next to a friend from Lincolnshire. It was a zesty spring day and the sun was igniting the tops of recently ploughed furrows, 'Just look at sun on that soil out there Spring; don't it make you want to get out and dig it!' Where Maureen lived, in the south of the county, the land is dissected by dykes holding back rivers straightened by the hands of men. Ominously many of these dykes are above the level of the land and so they carry the permanent threat that the sea might one day take back what had been stolen from it. In 1953 it almost did. In Lincolnshire over 200,000 acres of that rich black soil were flooded; three hundred and seven died in those storms. No wonder Lincolnshire people take life and land seriously.

I was in for a culture shock when we got to Fulton. Maureen lived with her parents in a terraced cottage. It had no indoor toilet and the only running water came from a standpipe in a scullery virtually unaltered since Victorian times. A narrow side door gave access to the living room which though small somehow managed to accommodate an open fire, a TV, two easy chairs, a dining table and three dining chairs. Next to this room was the 'posh' room only used for Sunday tea and other special occasions. Three bedrooms, up a steep enclosed staircase were larger, but on my first visit to this small, low-ceilinged house I felt like Lemuel Gulliver.

The Olivers were home owners, we had a council house; the Olivers were middle-class, we were emphatically working-class; yet we were financially better-off. What's more, we had a bathroom and a toilet and hot running water; the Oliver's toilet was down the garden, an earth closet, cleaned out once a quarter by the men with the violet cart. How had these conditions nurtured the elegant, sophisticated Maureen? Henry and Doreen Oliver didn't simply love and support their offspring – as our parents had James and me – but they lived for and through her. They sent her to primary school with a serviette in her lunch box. And she, an only child, ruled the house: I sensed that Doreen was a little afraid of her daughter.

If they were worse off than the Springs, and if Henry didn't ride to hounds after all, the Olivers still lived much better than we did. I hadn't encountered the pleasure of country food since I was a child; the quality and variety of this food far surpassed what I was used to. Moreover dinner was brought to the table in dishes whereas our meals were always ready-served on the plate. Doreen cooked breakfast every morning whereas I had Weetabix and toast and usually got it myself. The Olivers, I discovered, were rich in ways in which we were poor, and this came as a revelation. There was a modest sobriety about them that was quite foreign to me, though I admired it. I grew very fond of this new world where each day began with the comforting smell of bacon and tomatoes wafting up the stairs. I felt relaxed and confident in my relationship with the Olivers, especially their daughter.

One academic bonus that Mo brought unsolicited was a commendable work ethic, and I began to spend far more time in the library than ever and my essay marks began to benefit greatly. I got an A++ for one! Though neither I nor many of my friends had any firm ideas on future careers at this time, some were planning to take the post-graduate teaching certificate. This seemed a good scheme: the qualification might prove handy and, just as important, it would mean no separation from Mo, who still had another year to complete her degree. I signed up, with my parents' approval.

Towards the end of that term Stanley Walker, my Politics tutor with the doleful eyes, called me into his study. Would I be interested in continuing my studies by 'doing research'? What on earth was that? Walker explained that if I obtained a 'good' Upper Second Honours degree the Department would like me to work for a higher degree, researching a subject and writing up my findings in a thesis – a 'book' – of about 200 pages. Me writing a 'book'! Just considering the possibility made me glow. But what to research? Walker suggested I might research the Liberals. In March 1962 the party had won a stunning by-election victory in Orpington, a genuine bombshell. If ever there was a time to be writing about the Liberal party, now was it. All I needed was a good 2i. I could only hope that Malcolm Reece would have the decency to carry me over the line.

In my final year politics became important to me in a way that it hadn't before. I had come to university to study Politics only because I couldn't get admittance to a History programme on its own. Yes, I had an interest in politics: I was staunch Labour but now Harold Macmillan's was advising everyone to vote Conservative because his party could manage a socialist state better than Labour! Perhaps he was right, though I could hear my mate Trevor from Poplar Hospital on the Tories: 'I'm not saying they're always wrong, I just hate the bastards.' But the world *was* changing and old certainties were dying: in the US the recently elected President John F. Kennedy seemed to represent a new kind of politics. And who wasn't interested in politics in those days? The greatest issue of the day was the threat of nuclear war. Thousands of people of all ages, walks of life and political and religious persuasions marched from the nuclear weapons establishment at Aldermaston to Trafalgar Square each Easter to protest against nuclear weapons. Bertrand Russell demonstrated mathematically that nuclear war was certain: no wonder everyone was interested. And I spent my days studying these issues!

'Finals' were now upon us: the most important exams of our lives. As each exam came and went we would remove the relevant books from our shelves, the goal being a bare bookshelf. Halfway through I put all my books back: I really couldn't handle the thought of an empty bookshelf. In some of my Finals papers I was impossibly stretched; I hadn't even covered the work in the first place, let alone revised it: Mo and her work ethic had arrived too late. Nevertheless I managed my 'good' Upper Second and could now contemplate a fourth year at Sheffield: there was a Master's degree and a teaching diploma to occupy me and, just as important, a burgeoning relationship to foster. And since we were allowed only three years in Hall, there was the small matter of finding some accommodation.

For now though a little celebration was surely in order. Our degree results were published in the *Yorkshire Post* and my name appeared top of our class list, above even Malcolm Reece. The Springs and the Robsons were thrilled: they knew even less about degree classifications than I but seeing my name at the top of the list in the *Post* was more than good enough. I found a copy of the relevant page in my mum's photo drawer years later. I had repaid a little bit of the debt I owed them

Ch.4: *The End of the Beginning*

Ten Grantham Park was a handsome Edwardian villa about half a mile from Robertson. The house, our home for the next year, had been discovered by Butch Harris who had come up early to do the hunting and had managed it all with his customary quiet efficiency. It comprised three floors with an allegedly self-contained flat on each. Nathan, Butch and I would share the ground floor flat, Kieran, Philip and Gareth would take the second. The attic flat was inhabited by the statutory, and statuesque, blond. No Bella Mason, but you did feel that anyone invited up for the evening would be lucky to escape intact.

The set-up was ideal for us Robertsonians because the six of us could easily cooperate in using the one decent kitchen. There was a good-sized television in the downstairs lounge, with enough seating for six. Part of the lounge had been walled off, creating an additional bedroom. This was the land of Butch. Nathan and I had a room that, with its dual-function table, trebled up as bed room, dining room and billiard room. The second floor was similar if not so grand but all the larger rooms had gas fires, central heating having gone out of fashion with the departure of the Romans. The house belonged to an odd couple, Ted and Sandra, who claimed to be siblings from a close-knit family. They visited reasonably frequently to 'work on their books' in a small office on the second floor and once Gareth, having knocked on the door without response, put his head in only to discover Ted and Sandra knitting very closely indeed.

Andy and Robbie had gone their own way by now. They were in a house further out of town, and we in No.10 saw little of them.

However, we did see a lot of another Old Robertsonian, Don Clarke. Short and thick-set Don had played full-back for the University rugby team and his bravery was legendary. Throughout his undergraduate days Don had maintained a close relationship with his childhood sweetheart, subsequently his wife. He had secured a teaching post in Sheffield to be taken up after graduation and Eileen had the promise of a job in a shoe shop in the centre of town. They had got themselves a flat in a large and elegant Victorian house and were to be married that summer. Except Don didn't graduate. His degree, like Mo's, comprised three subjects and was specifically structured for those intending to become teachers. He achieved a pass in all of his twelve papers but he failed the 'unseen' section of one of the French papers, which meant a failure overall in that paper. And a failed paper meant a failed degree. Don had to resit all four French papers the following year, despite having already unequivocally passed three. These days a university operating such a mediaeval system would be burned down by the students. Sitting in my room in Robertson after the results came out this man among men broke down and cried. He got his degree the next summer, but in the meantime taught unqualified and was paid less than his new wife in the shoe shop.

We saw a lot of Don at No.10 that year because I'd undertaken to teach him to swim, something he'd never managed before because, unlike the rest of the entire animal kingdom, he couldn't float. Of course this is not possible but Don didn't seem to know that. I eventually managed to help him to the stage where he no longer sank, or even expected to sink, though this was the consequence of my explaining how to achieve minimum momentum. Nevertheless we had constructed a foundation and the following year, finally qualified and back home teaching in Lincolnshire, Don got his 100 yards certificate at his new school. Half the school turned out to cheer him on. He was that sort of bloke.

In the meantime we at No.10 had to come to terms with the education diploma. What redeemed the year was the actual teaching practice. For would-be secondary teachers like us the first practice comprised two weeks in a primary school followed by two five-week practices in secondary schools, grammar and modern. My primary practice was in Rotherham where I encountered the word 'gerrodenim'. It came up in a boy's composition. Was it a verb, a noun, an adjective, a bird, a plane – or what? I asked the little lad who had used the word what it meant. 'Wha's tha' mean sir?' he replied totally at a loss, 'it's just...gerrodenim.' So I asked him to use the word just as he would in real life. 'See thee sir, if our kid was to give us a slap I'd run after 'im, gerrodenim and pan 'im one back.' Get hold of him, see? Simples!

That October we experienced the Cuban Missile Crisis. This face-off between President Kennedy and the Russian leader Nikita Khrushchev over the siting of Russian nuclear weapons on Cuba looked to be heading for a nuclear war as neither side seemed willing to back down. My mum phoned one evening and suggested that she and my dad transfer their savings to my account in Sheffield: London would surely be destroyed. I pointed out that the whole country would be blown to smithereens; anyway, she wasn't to worry I said with very little confidence, it would soon all blow over. It did, but all the same it was eerie, trying to continue day-to-day living – who'd used the last of the marmalade? – in the face of the possible extermination of the human species and its entire stock of marmalade. Yorkshire's Early-Warning System at Fylingdales was still under construction but just about able to give us four minutes notice of our extinction. Enough time, as The Dubliners sang, to bend down and kiss your bum goodbye. Well thank God war didn't ensue, though on the debit side, Irish bums were never to know the affection in which they were held.

Later that autumn another phenomenon, coming from nowhere, threatened to destroy the British establishment: the late-night satirical show *That Was The Week That Was*. We would gather round the set in the lounge each Saturday with a few beers and watched our politicians pilloried. Prime Minister Macmillan – Supermac – was the chief target: suddenly he looked like an old man at the mercy of 'events, dear boy, events'. *TW3* didn't engineer the change in public perception of the Tory government, indeed of politicians generally, but it surely gave it legs.

Towards the end of November 1962 it started to snow, trapping the newly fallen leaves. It became increasingly cold as December wore on and at the end of the month there were more heavy snowfalls throughout the country. On Boxing Day the heavens opened and a strong wind brought drifts of twenty feet in many places, especially on the Yorkshire Wolds. Mo and I had to change our plans. It made no sense for her to travel down to London where things were so bad that my parents had to cancel their New Year party for the first time. When I got back to Sheffield in January the cold was knife sharp, though No.10 was warm enough. Winter or no winter, our second teaching placement was to be taken early in that new term. The comrades were flung far and wide, but not me: I was posted to King Alfred's, two hundred yards down the road. They all trudged off into the snow in the early hours while I enjoyed a leisurely piece of toast by the gas fire.

King Alfred's was a grammar school much like my own but apart from its convenience I didn't enjoy the placement. Few of the staff found time to chat to the trainees or to make us welcome. I was taken under the wing of a rather unprepossessing middle-aged History teacher from Buckinghamshire who made it clear that he didn't think I was up to teaching in a good grammar school, but he did allow me to teach one session of Politics to the fourth-years. He sat right at the front and watched me minutely. Towards the end of the class one of the students asked which constituency the Prime Minister Harold Macmillan represented. I knew this as well as I knew who opened the batting for Yorkshire, but that malignant presence in the front seat seemed to will me to forget and I did. Meanwhile Mr. Smallmind was whispering something to me which I couldn't catch so, apologising to the class that it has slipped my mind, I asked my nemesis did he know? He almost spat out 'Bromley!' After the lesson Mr. Smug roasted me. It was totally unprofessional to admit to a class that you didn't know something you ought to have known. I begged to differ, which turned out to be about as good a move as sounding a klaxon in an Alpine valley prone to avalanches.

It was around this time that Ted and Sandra explained that they were going to have to invest in a cat; mice had been discovered in No.10. Two days later a sweet little tortoise-shell creature appeared, hardly bigger than the mice he was being deployed to terrorise. He would come and lie out in front of the gas fire of an evening and when nicely warmed, favour Nathan by leaping onto his lap. Nathan spent ages playing with him. He attached a metal ring to the end of a piece of cord and would dangle it in front of the kitten, which would rise up on his hind legs and biff the ring rather like a boxer with a punch-ball. It wasn't long before we discovered that he had fleas. Now at the time Nathan had a beautiful girlfriend of whom we were all a little bit enamoured. A few years older than us Sophie was elegantly, mysteriously French. They were falling in love, Nathan and Sophie, and this gave pleasure to us all. Now amongst her very many attributes, she knew about cats and the first thing she did on being introduced to Sam the kitten was to explore his fur. One evening she sat in front of the gas fire cracking fleas until she felt able to declare young Sam a flea-free zone. Later on she did the same for Nathan; at least, that's what it sounded like from the TV room.

Then one day about three weeks later Sam went missing. After two days of no Sam we reported his absence to Ted and Sandra, who informed the police. The next day Nathan answered a call from Her Majesty's Constabulary down at Hunter's Bar. A cat answering Sam's description had been found. Hang on, said Nathan, we're talking kittens here, not cats. Oh no, they said, this'll be the fellah. About dinner time two officers appeared at the door with a cylindrical container. They would just let him out into the hall, they said. As they opened the catch, a tortoise-shell object exploded past Nathan and shot off down the hall. When he turned back to explain to the officers that this creature was to our Sam as Boadicea might have been to Little Nell, they had legged it, one calling back over his shoulder that, 'Yon's a reight good mouser, pal. He'll be fine.'

The beast was ferocious and it was clear to all that no *modus vivendi* was on the cards. Clear to all except Nathan who tried to befriend it that first evening. Out came his metal-ring-at-the-end-of-bit-of-cord and he twirled it in front of our new companion and invited him to play. This feline Samson took a step forward and delivered the ring such a clout that the cord snapped and the metal ring flew off in the general direction of Jupiter. This wasn't so much a cat as a Jabberwock. He stayed for three days and his departure was just as sudden as his arrival. One morning Butch, in his dressing gown, went to bring in the milk. Glimpsing the chink of light over his shoulder the Jabberwock took off like an Exocet, pitching Butch into the snow. Frabjous – we never saw him again! To be fair neither did we see any further evidence of mice for the rest of our stay at No.10. Not bad for three days work!

March, still in the grip of winter, brought our final practice. I had to go to a secondary modern school in Rotherham. The Head turned out to be quietly spoken and in his late fifties and he wore an academic gown. In a Secondary Modern? In Rotherham? Then I got to meet Thorpe the History teacher and I understood. He was a head shorter than me but much thicker set and he carried about him an air of menace that I hadn't encountered since my adolescent days on the Isle of Dogs. His baleful eyes communicated malevolence; his way of speaking was distilled scorn and his questions razor blades. Imagine the love child of Genghis Khan and Lucrezia Borgia with the looks of Caliban. He it was who set the tone of the school.

Two lessons from this five-week period in Rotherham would remain with me for the rest of my life. The first was one that I myself taught, and it was memorable because it went so well. It

43

was formally 'observed' by my tutor, a tall, bony American woman from the South called Layne – we christened her Bronco. The lesson was about how to write a short story. I borrowed a Gurkha's kukri from Butch, whose bedroom wall it adorned, and an umbrella from Kieran. I showed the class the umbrella then told them a story about it, and explained how I'd structured the story, what style of writing I'd employed and so on, and then I invited them to write their own story. At that point I produced the kukri. And here 'inspiration' took over: I threw it into the wooden floorboards, where it stuck. 'Now write a story about that knife,' I said with what I like to think was a flourish and sat down. They were stunned. Bronco was stunned. Told me off later, mind, for damaging school property.

The second memorable lesson came towards the end of the placement. There was a lad in the fifth year called Syme who was appropriately known as Slime. He wasn't part of any group; even the class villains, amongst whom he sat, wanted nothing to do with him. Now Thorpe, who in fairness had no favourites – he hated them all equally – had a set-to with Syme in the last period before lunch, when Syme, accused of some misdemeanour, blamed it on the fact that he was being victimised by the villains. Come lunchtime there was more trouble involving Syme in the queue; a group of girls called over to Thorpe, who was in charge, saying that 'Slimey' was trying to push in. Thorpe sent him to the back of the queue where the villains happened to be skulking. More trouble. Again Syme complained about victimisation. Over lunch the villains decided that if it was victimisation he wanted victimisation he would get. They forced Syme into one of the rubbish bins in the playground and fixed the lid on. The lid was removed a minute or so later and, if Syme is to be believed, some of them peed on him. He ran off home and told his out-of-work dad that Thorpe had organised all this and so dad, fortified by a few Johnnie Walkers, marched up to the school to unseat tyranny.

The first period of the afternoon had just began, Syme-less, when this gentleman – unmistakably the progenitor of young Master Syme – stormed into the room effing-and-blinding, making straight for Thorpe. Whilst explaining that he would prefer to hold the conversation outside, Thorpe managed to propel Syme senior back through the door without, so I would have sworn, the latter's feet touching the ground. The effing and blinding resumed only briefly in the corridor; it was ground remorselessly down by a voice of incredible resonance and ferocity in which the character defects of young Master Syme were itemised in considerable detail. Thorpe declared that he wouldn't have demeaned himself by giving even a moment's thought to the boy in question, let alone arranging for his punishment by others. Moreover, he concluded, with almost Shakespearean eloquence, from what he knew of young Syme's character he ought to consider himself lucky they didn't shit on him. Syme senior was then projected towards the exit, utterly vanquished.

The Spring Term had been a productive one for Mo and me. She had been working conscientiously preparing for her Finals and I had been researching the Liberal party: indeed I had completed all the background reading and even arranged a number of interviews with prominent party members for the Easter holidays. Mo was to come down to London for a few days and I was to take another trip to Lincolnshire. Before that, though, on the last Saturday of term, was the small business of Mo's twenty-first birthday party: it was then that we announced our engagement. We had been assiduously collecting thre'penny joeys for about a year and together these little chaps provided just about enough for a ring with several small rubies in a diamond setting. When we had discussed our future in that bleakest of mid-winters I had floated the idea of buying a motor bike so that when Mo had graduated and I had completed my training, we might save up a pannier full of joeys and take off around Europe. Mo's response? If I thought she would slum it round Europe on a bike ridden by a man who had manifestly demonstrated an inability to manage one, I'd better think again. Travel was OK but I would need to upgrade. Quite serendipitously the following week I saw an advert on the departmental notice board for Commonwealth Scholarships. That very day I applied for one to go to New Zealand. Mo was OK with that.

My Easter break research interviews went well, the best was with Lady Violet Bonham Carter, Asquith's daughter. She invited me to her London apartment and was informative and entertaining, but her opening question rattled me: how did I take my tea, green or black? *Green* tea? How long have you had the stuff?

I was called for interview by the Commonwealth Scholarships Board in London. Looking at the map on the wall at King's Cross Underground station when I arrived I saw that the Jubilee Line would take me very close to where I needed to be. Over half an hour later I enquired when the next Jubilee Line train was due. In approximately fifteen years came the answer! Mortified I arrived thirty minutes late and was pleasantly surprised to be seen, and even more surprised at how well the interview seemed to go. A week later a letter arrived offering me a Research Scholarship for three years in Wellington beginning in autumn 1964. If successful I would gain a PhD, something I'd never even heard of the year before. Surely *then* an opening in politics would appear, maybe with the Liberal party?

The term hadn't gone so well for Nathan. His love affair with the wonderful Sophie had sustained him through a very difficult time with his teacher-training. He was a conscientious trainee teacher – in fact he was conscientious about most things – but he was not naturally blessed with luck and his supervisor seemed to have taken against him. She set out to make his life a misery but Nathan was a strong guy. What brought him down was Sophie. He wanted to take her home to meet the family because he planned to marry her. His parents responded by pointing out that any gentile friend would be made most welcome in the house – as indeed I had been – but that if he were intending to marry a gentile, she would never be welcome: he would be on his own. Nathan was devastated: he knew that it was not in his power to separate himself from his family, his home, his culture. What would he have left to offer Sophie? So after weeks on the rack he knew he had to break with her. He was heartbroken; in fact we were all bereft.

Sheffield days were coming to an end. Maureen graduated with flying colours; discovering the results, she dissolved in tears of joy and relief in the main road, and right next to a workmen's hut, threw her arms round me and kissed me. Most un-Mo like! That particular hut, would you believe, was full of the guys I'd worked with the year before. What a reception we got! Meanwhile Mo had managed to find a teaching post in Spalding, near to her old school, and was to teach for the last weeks of term and be paid over the summer. This was a coup. No more working at Butlin's! As for me, I had a degree, a teaching certificate, and a half-completed MA thesis to my name, and plans were being laid to marry a year later and sail off to New Zealand for three years. But no job!

Our group planned one last holiday together, camping on Corsica. No hitching this time. We had a superb couple of weeks on the island, though the sun gave us no mercy. The comrades left at different times till only Mo and I remained. On our last evening we sat looking over the Mediterranean from the hills above Ajaccio as the sun went down and at the horizon the sky and sea as they met went first gold, then orange, then crimson, then purple and finally black. So it really was all over! Sheffield had been good to me. Very good. Times might be just as good in the future, but surely never better. Now each of the comrades was about to launch himself into the unpredictable waters of the real world. Though we would go our different ways the friendships we had built and shared over the previous four years would remain strong and last for the whole of our lives. But then, what would you have expected from something forged in Sheffield?

Ch.5: *Gi's a Job!*

The level of noise as I entered the classroom unnerved me. I raised my voice, told them who I was and that I had come to teach them History: I needed to know where they had left off last year. Left off what, they asked? I tried again: 'What were you doing last year in History?' All hell broke loose. Desk lids were thumped; the massive iron windows were thrown open and banged shut; boys hanging down from frames. Totally humiliated, I sat down, waiting for a senior staff member to come and rescue me. But nobody came: I was on my own. Of all my life experiences that double lesson with 3B on Tuesday 10th September, only three weeks after Corsica, turned out to be one of the most intimidating. Slowly something like sanity began to return. 'Thank you! What was that all about?' A sharp-featured lad at the front of the class replied: 'Well, you asked us what we was doin' last year in 'Istry. That's what we was doin'.' 'OK... well this year we won't be doing that. We're going to be doing the Tudors.' Universal groan. 'Why?' somebody called out. 'Well, look,' I began, 'you're lucky enough to live in a beautiful city with famous buildings that go back hundreds of years to the Tudors and even earlier. Only natural you'd want to find out about them and the people who lived there, right?' 'Na!' 'Listen, they *belong* to you. They're interesting.' 'No they en't, they're borin.' 'OK,' I said, on another tack, 'you learn History to pass examinations. You pass examinations, you get qualifications, you get a good job.' ''Ere, sir, my dad works in the brick yards – bet 'e earns more'n you. Waste er time, qualifications.' Was Elvis Presley a scholar? Did Bobby Charlton pass the Eleven Plus? This was the

New World. 'Well, listen, you're going to study Tudor History because *I say you will*, and that's all there is to it,' I barked. 'Now get your pencils and exercise books out and take some notes.' This was a technique I had acquired during training: to establish order, get the sods to do some dictation. I saw a TV drama in which a new English teacher asked his class in a London comprehensive what they'd been doing the previous year. *Hard Times,* they replied. But what *exactly*? 'We was copyin' it out!' In mitigation, it is one of Dickens's shorter works.

Ten minutes later when those without books had been given books and those without pencils had been given pencils, I dictated some notes by way of introduction to the Tudors. After about five minutes that sharp-eyed lad put his hand up. 'Please sir, I med a mistake.' 'What's your name?' I asked. 'Lesek, sir,' he replied. 'So rub it out Lesek.' 'Please sir, I 'ent got no rubba'.' 'Can anyone lend this boy a rubber?' I asked. 'I got one sir,' said a lad from the back and out he came, to wide applause, wafting a used contraceptive. We hadn't covered this in the teacher-training programme last year. My final indignity, as the lesson ended, was being asked by one young gentleman if I was Swedish. I talked funny.

I might have guessed from the start that Tuesday 10th of September wasn't going to be my day. As I had made my way to the rear entrance of the school I had been hailed by a very large red-faced man with wispy grey hair loitering at the main entrance. 'Boy!' he bellowed, 'get round to the main entrance immediately. You're late.' What could I say? I ignored the man, who then came bounding after me. 'Didn't you 'ear me, boy?' he shouted at my back. I turned. 'Good morning. I'm a new colleague of yours.' A look of enlightenment slowly melted his grim mask into a smile.

'OK. I'll let you off this time! Name's Thompson,' he added, smiling and offering a huge hand.

Nobody in the staff room seemed much interested in me when I appeared and I hung about like a lost soul. Then I committed the classical crime of *lèse majesté* by sitting in a seat which apparently belonged to a large Geography teacher whose proprietary rights were no doubt recorded in the Domesday Book. He curtly demanded that I move; I slunk away sheepishly. Years later Kieran would strike a blow for all who had been similarly humiliated. He'd been invited to a local school to advise on further education opportunities. Whilst his host was getting him a coffee a tweedy mound of belligerence hovered in front of him. 'Mind movin' yourself? You're in my chair,' it hissed. Kieran looked up. 'Sod off,' he replied and returned to his *Guardian*. The mound erupted.

An appointment with the Headmaster had been arranged for me during the morning break, after my double lesson, and it turned out to be most helpful. A softly spoken Welshman; his words carried conviction. He provided me with a black size 13 sandshoe and strongly advised me to make use of it, especially with 3B, who, he agreed, were notorious. 'You got to get on top of them boy, and if that means a bit of slipperin', then slipper! It's you or them. And when you're on top, you can ease off. No good appealin' to reason with 3B. With 3B it's the slipper. Anyway, punishment's good for 'em in the long run, to be honest with you. It's all there in *Hebrews XII* verses 11-13. Look it up, boy.' Just what I needed: a strategy for survival ordained by scripture and the tool to do the job!

But how had I got myself into this fix in the first place? With my BA (Hons) in History and Politics and my post-graduate

Diploma in Education I'd duly set out to conquer the world that summer. But how – and where? Proximity to Mo was crucial, since we had to plan our stay in New Zealand, not to mention our wedding. I decided to write to the Education Office in Peterborough, the largest urban area near to Mo's home. In my letter I stressed that I would prefer not to teach to A Level since I was completing a Master's and needed to minimise time spent on preparation. Ideally I would like to teach History to O Level and coach soccer or rugby. I received a reply calling me for interview on the Wednesday before term was due to start.

That visit to Peterborough was my first and there was no love at first sight. The education offices were housed in a soulless modern building and after a short wait I was ushered into the cramped office of a middle-aged man who was much too big for it. Sniffing disdainfully he rose, hung out a limp hand, sat down again, took out my letter and proffered me a chair. Without looking up he asked: 'So you're after a job with the Authority.' Drumming of inky fingers. 'What exactly were you lookin' for?' So I told him. 'Yeah, that's what it says here: History and football or rugby.' 'Well, ideally,' I said helpfully. 'Right,' he concluded, closing the file without looking up. 'Start Sleaford Road Toosday.' 'Doing what exactly?' Now he looked up, eyebrows arched feigning surprise, 'History in the mornin's, sport in the afternoons of a Monday, Wednesday and Friday. Right? You'll be in charge of the football team.' 'Right!' I said, then almost as an afterthought: 'Can you tell me where Sleaford Road *is*, and can you give any advice about finding digs?' 'Yeah,' he said, 'see my sec'try. Close the door after you.' With secretarial advice I managed both to locate the school and find suitable digs. The deal included no option to stay over at the weekends but that suited me.

Thanks to my newly acquired driving license I would drive over and spend most weekends with Mo and the Olivers – once I had a car!

The 1960s saw a significant increase in the number of drivers on British roads, including both my parents. This constituted a revolutionary change to their way of life, as it did to many working-class families at the time. I too had passed my test and Henry Oliver, a man with contacts in the trade, had helpfully located a grey Morris Minor for sale at £150, which he thought would be just the job for me. I had been offered a loan from the local bank in Fulton provided I got myself a job. So, with the school term fast approaching, I'd planned to leave No.12, where I'd been staying since my interview, on the Friday morning, take the train up to Fulton, sort out my bank loan in the afternoon and purchase the car the next day. Then on Monday evening I would drive over to Peterborough ready to begin work at the school on the Tuesday. Simples! Thereafter I would be able to motor over to the Olivers Friday evenings and drive back early the following Monday morning.

On Saturday morning Henry took Mo and me down to the garage, where the Morris Minor had been tarted up and was waiting coyly. Forms signed, cheque delivered and hands shaken we took the car out for a maiden run with Henry driving, listening appreciatively to the engine tone and putting the car through its paces. We parked up in time for lunch, with a view to having a spin on our own in the afternoon.

I can't describe the pride with which I brandished the key that afternoon, letting Mo in and then climbing in myself, adjusting the position and rake of the seat and putting the key confidently in the ignition. I sat for a brief while taking this moment in. The little lad who had been almost borne off by a band of marauding poultices twenty or so years earlier in Ripon was now a professional with a job, a bank account, a fiancée and a car. I took a deep breath, smiled confidently at Mo and turned the key. Nothing. I tried again; again the starter motor whirred but failed to spur the engine into life. A third failure brought home to me the sad fact that my world hadn't really changed that much after all: time to call for a proper grown-up. Henry soon ascertained that the starter motor was missing some teeth but only needed to be advanced slightly to engage. So at last we were able to speed out into the fens, with me driving gingerly at first but with growing confidence. On Monday I would drive to Peterborough alone in the dark, a journey I'd never made by road. Cometh the hour I was quietly terrified and almost shat myself. Ensconced finally in my digs I slept not a wink. Thank goodness I'd no intimation of what lay ahead the next morning.

After three or four weeks at Sleaford Road I managed to tame most of the trouble-makers in 3B with the help of the sandshoe, but not Lesek. For him I had to devise something else. He was a dynamic midfielder in the First Eleven, and under my direction the team has started the season well. A big game against local rivals was fixed for Wednesday. Lesek was an absolute pain that Tuesday and at the end of the lesson I told him to report at the sports pavilion at 2.15pm. 'But sir, that's kick-off time gen Eastfield,' he complained. 'Better not be late then,' I replied. Lesek duly appeared, all kitted out, at 2.15pm on the dot. I told him what I expected, and what I wouldn't tolerate: did we have an understanding? 'Yeah, yeah; can I go now, sir?' 'OK Lesek – but first run round the games field – twice. I'll be watching you, mind.' 'But we're playin' wi' ten men, sir, *gen Eastfield!*' 'Right. And whose fault's that?' By and large that was the last of my problems with Lesek.

Except once. The school Art master had taught me how to throw pots and I would often spend an hour or so at the end of the school day at the wheel. I loved it and in fact made several pots that still adorn lesser visited parts of our house. My masterpiece was a tea pot. Difficult: it has four pieces thrown or pulled individually: the chamber, the spout, the handle and the lid. I had a number of failures, but was finally satisfied – besotted might be better. The completed tea pot was then placed on the cupboard shelf ready to be biscuit fired before glazing. So impressed was the Art master that he showed it to his next class that afternoon: 3B.

I was clearing my desk at the end at the day when Lesek came in, walked past me without a word, straight over to the cupboard where the dreaded 'slipper' was kept. He came back with the slipper. 'You're gonna need this, sir,' he said, placing it almost reverently on the desk. I looked up. 'I'm real sorry sir...but I've gone an' smashed your tea pot. See, I thought it were great, sir, an' I took it off the shelf to look...I thought it were biscuit...but it weren't...the 'andle came off an' the pot smashed on the floor. Sir...I'm right sorry.' And he really was; just not as sorry as me. 'Lesek, get the Hell out of here before I bloody biscuit fire *you!*' I'd never be able to bring it off again – ever. I drove over to Fulton after tea to be consoled by Mo only to discover that she was out – insult to injury – at a Tupperware party.

Spending the weekends with the Olivers helped keep me grounded that year. I never took school work or research work with me, so there was always time to relax, to think and to read.

55

On Friday nights I'd have a jar with Henry at the Constitutional Club. On Saturdays Mo and I would go out somewhere, and on Sunday mornings I would take myself off to the Methodist chapel where the local Catholics held Mass: not many in this part of the world – Cromwell country – but our numbers were augmented by Italian fruit pickers and bottlers who came over for the summer season. Earlier that year the Anglican Bishop of Woolwich, John Robinson, had caused a furore by rejecting the traditional view of God as the Supreme Being and redefining Him instead as Pure Love: inside us down here, not outside us up there. I found this compelling but wanted the best of both worlds: to hold on to the traditions of a strong community based on the teaching of Christ and yet to bring things up to date. John XXIII had set up the Second Vatican Council in 1961 to do pretty much that. Coincidentally one of its reforms was the Mass itself. I had recently mastered the Latin Mass: now it was about to be replaced by the vernacular. Just like ballroom dancing; by the time I'd mastered it, it was done away with.

Not all weekends followed this pattern: we missed our Friday night drink on November 22nd, the night Kennedy was assassinated, and spent the weekend in a daze. Half a dozen times during the year Mo and I went to Sheffield for the weekend and I would spend an hour or two on the Friday evening discussing progress on my dissertation with my tutor Stanley Walker. Our last weekend visit to Sheffield was scheduled for a Friday in early July when we were to discuss my completed first draft. That happened to be the day of the annual staff v boys cricket match. I had already explained to Hanson, the senior games teacher at the beginning of term that I had never played cricket and was unqualified to offer anything other than my presence on games afternoons, so I was surprised to be asked to play. When it transpired that the game was to be played on the day we were heading for Sheffield for my crucial meeting, I told Hanson I wouldn't be able to make it. On the morning in question my name nevertheless appeared on the team sheet – opening the batting!

Later I discovered that Hanson had run the football team for years and had been shunted aside to make way for me. His bitterness was exacerbated by the team's comparative success. Now there were two fast bowlers at the school who had represented Northamptonshire Schools and the prospect of them stitching up his nemesis warmed his heart. I reminded him forcefully of my complete lack of experience and my of time constraints: I should *have* to leave for Sheffield at 4pm latest. Hanson assured me this wouldn't be a problem.

On a balmy Friday afternoon made for cricket a coin was tossed and a match begun. The boys won the toss and decided to bat first. They were finally all out just before 3.30pm. At 3.45pm the Chemistry teacher and I went in to bat, the former in his whites. Somehow I managed to survive for three overs of very fast bowling without being hit. I even managed to get on top of one steeply rising ball and glance it for four in the first over and, coming forward, clubbed another through the covers for four in the third. I was quite enjoying myself, though I found it impossible to gauge when it was safe to run a single and missed several good opportunities. Halfway through the fifth over I received a spitting delivery that moved in off the seam and went straight through me, clattering the stumps. Hanson was umpiring at square leg and I had to pass him on the way back to the pavilion. Just as I did so the clock struck 4pm 'You *bastard* Spring!' he spat with venom. He had somehow conceived the idea that I was actually a very competent cricketer – didn't my cleanly struck boundaries prove it? – and I had chosen to stay just long enough to demonstrate my prowess whilst disdaining easily available singles. At *exactly* 4pm, just to spite him, I had surrendered my wicket, neatly turning the tables on him!

I could count my year at Sleaford Road a success. Six of the seven in my O Level class passed, three with 'B's. A visiting educational officer happened to be in the Headmaster's office when I went to say goodbye. They told me that my year's probation had been successfully completed. 'There will always be room for you in this authority, lad,' said the official. 'Don't forget us when you get back.' I was gratified, though most of the credit should have gone to a size 13 sandshoe. I never warmed to Peterborough, even when I saw a well-endowed young woman walking topless down Queensgate. In addition to my teaching I had finished the first draft of my Master's. I owed Walker a lot – more even than I realised. Much later I discovered that he had paid my registration fees.

In the last week of term the younger members of Sleaford Road staff room drove out into Leicestershire for a celebratory drink and to wish me luck: the following week we were to be married and two days later off to New Zealand. On our way back raucous and indecent singing shattered the silence of several Leicestershire and Northamptonshire villages. Next day I drove down to No.12 for a couple of days at home. The following afternoon two detectives knocked on the door of No.12 and asked if I were the owner of the grey Morris Minor in the street. What, they asked suspiciously, had I been doing in Leicestershire around midnight two nights before? Surely we hadn't been *that* noisy? It transpired that a robbery had taken place in one of the villages and my car had been seen in the vicinity. The detectives seemed satisfied with my explanation but as they left: 'Can we take it that you won't be leaving the country in the next few days, sir?' 'Well, officer, as it happens, in four days from now...'

That night James, Kieran and I went for a quiet Bachelor's Night in *The Gun*, down on the river. I reflected that this might be my last sight of it: sweet Thames run softly till I end my song. Next morning a fleet of Springs, Robsons, assorted aunts, uncles and cousins took the A11 out of East London heading for the Lincolnshire fens and the nuptials of Maureen Anne Oliver and Thomas Daniel Spring, prior to the transportation of said couple to the colonies.

Ch.6: *The Lure of the South*

A globe of sweat travelled inexorably from the priest's forehead to the tip of his nose where it hung as if by magic off the end of the clerical proboscis before dropping with an audible splat onto his bible, open at the Marriage Service. The temperature registered 84 degrees in Oldspeak on the afternoon of August 5th 1964, at St. Mark's, Fulton. Maureen Oliver, in her elegant, white wedding gown, fruit of her own labour, was in the process of becoming Mrs. Maureen Spring and at that very moment was vowing to love, cherish and obey her husband-to-be. The church was full of friends and family. The organ was played in some style by the Music teacher at Sleaford Road, principal organist at Peterborough Cathedral.

The reception was held just over the road and we had around sixty guests. Everything went as it should and although Mo carried it all off serenely I was like a fish out of water. Apart from my brief introduction to ballroom dancing, I had received few lessons in how to function socially. True I was taught the knack of eating peas off the back of my fork, as one does in polite circles, but how to handle myself on social occasions not involving peas? Nothing! So on what should have been my day of days I was only at ease when finally we drove off, tin cans clanking and balloons bouncing, to spend our wedding night in a big old Norfolk coaching inn.

We stayed the next night with Henry and Doreen before leaving the following day for London. No tears on the platform at King's Lynn; perhaps they would have helped. We stayed overnight at No.12 and on the Friday the four of us, with James, drove to Tilbury to board the *RMV Rangitane*. One of my dad's many cousins worked for the New Zealand Shipping Company and he came down especially to show us around; the chef, he said, was the best on the line. Eventually it was time for the senior Springs to take their leave. Stiff upper lips again, though James wrote later that my mum had cried all weekend. The Springs believed they would probably never see their son and his new wife again.

Bunk beds are not the best sleeping arrangement for newly-weds on their honeymoon but on the whole the cabin was comfortable. We were to share a table with a delightful couple from County Down. Dennis was a Presbyterian minister on his way to a South Island parish and Elizabeth was a nurse. With that first meal it was easy to believe that ours was the line's best chef. We were to encounter a wide range of the best of food on the *Rangitane*, food such as we'd never experienced before, nor even knew existed. The New Zealand Shipping Company sailed home via the Panama Canal with only three stop-overs, at Curaçao in the Dutch West Indies, Panama City and Tahiti. Although the *Rangitane* wasn't a cruise ship it had a small but comfortable library, a music room, a ballroom and a small outdoor pool. Various deck activities were organised along with a chess championship and a deck tennis championship. Time passed easily. We were at sea for well over a week before reaching Curaçao and Mo had spent the first three days with a skin tone of a rather fetching green. Curaçao offered little beyond its splendid Dutch colonial architecture but our stay in Panama City was far more exciting. A few months previously the US embassy had been burned down, and the captain instructed us to travel mob-handed going into town and to take taxis everywhere. Dennis and Elizabeth had got to know another couple: Ralph was an archetypal Kiwi, tall, raw-boned and taciturn. He had been in the UK for three years and had met and wooed Lesley, a bouncy woman from Leeds. They were going to make their home in New Zealand. Ralph claimed some knowledge of the night scene in Panama City and enquired if we liked folk music. We all did except Mo, who pretended to. So Ralph undertook to show us a very atmospheric folk club he had visited on the way out.

The expression on the cab driver's face when Ralph mentioned our destination made me uneasy and when we got out of his cab I understood. There were two bulky gentlemen on the door and they were not selling *War Cry*. The first round of drinks cost an arm and more legs than you could shake a leg at and after we'd sat down a young woman appeared on a dais right in front of us and started to dance: it was a strip joint! Being confronted by a young lady baring her ample all right in front of you when what you were expecting was a hairy middle-aged geezer with a banjo and a mouth-organ can be quite off-putting, especially when escorting a brand new wife and in the company of a Presbyterian minister from County Down. 'She fancies you Tom,' Elizabeth giggled and sure enough I got a wink as two shapely breasts emerged. The last garment fell to a strangulated collective gasp from our table; unmistakably it revealed a willy, a todger, a Little Brother. She was a chap! 'Jeez,' said Ralph, 'I don't remember him from last time!'

On the third day in the Pacific we were hit by a storm, the second of the trip. In the first we had had lost power for thirty-six hours. This second storm was briefer but more violent, causing havoc in the middle of a Scottish country dancing lesson. Our final port of call was Papeete, capital of Tahiti. Gauguin had made a good job selling this rather dismal, down-at-heel place; though to be fair we saw little of the rest of the island. Before long we got a view of the sinewy East Coast of the North Island. We would be landing in Wellington in the evening of the next day. Mo had received a telegram offering her a teaching post at Wellington High School, which was a relief, and I had received one from the Head of the Political Science Department offering to meet us off the ship.

About 6.30 in the evening of Tuesday September 15th we came down the gangway and stood on New Zealand soil. A rather unprepossessing man in a grey raincoat and trilby hat stood on the concourse holding up a piece of cardboard with the barely discernible names 'Mr. and Mrs. Spring'. Richard Brooker explained that a departmental meeting had been arranged for the Thursday, but that next morning a man from the Accommodation Office would show us some flats. We walked about half a mile to a guest house on Willis Street. Brooker didn't offer to help with the cases; I don't think it occurred to him.

A nice cosy pub would have provided the perfect end to our first evening in NZ. Fat chance – pubs closed at six o'clock. We walked back the way we had come, down Willis Street and all the way along Lambton Quay to Parliament. This was the centre of New Zealand's capital city. Only one establishment was open and it sold milkshakes. Wellington felt not so much like another country as a parallel universe. Back at the guest house we found a key in the front door. I handed it in to the proprietor, who looked somewhat peeved. 'Course the key's still in the lock, mate; how else will guests get back in?'

Next morning the accommodation officer, a wiry Liverpudlian, explained that accommodation in Wellington was a major problem. He drove us up Te Aro Street through wooden down-at-heel houses with corrugated iron roofs, up to the top of Kelburn Parade where the houses became bigger and smarter with spectacular views over the harbour. We pulled up at the base of a steep incline, above which nestled three houses. 'Oh!' the accommodation officer observed, 'it's on the fault line!' Before I had time to ask what a fault line was the front doorbell had been answered by a slender, elegantly dressed woman in her seventies who welcomed us warmly. Mrs. Edna Mayfield was a third generation New Zealander, a retired school teacher who lived alone. We would share the kitchen and the bathroom and have a small living room and large bedroom to ourselves. The bedroom looked out to the open sea beyond the harbour mouth. The living room was tiny. We were advised that this place was far superior to the others and were persuaded to take it. We moved in on the Friday by which time I had discovered what a fault line was. I had had no idea that New Zealand suffered from earthquakes, still less that much of the centre of modern Wellington was built on land that had been thrust up out of the sea in 1853.

Before then was my meeting with the Department of Political Science. My expertise regarding third parties in a 'two-party' system, the subject of my Master's thesis would be useful in this new setting, very similar to Britain, or so Professor Brooker had written the previous March. Later in the year he wrote again, enquiring if I'd given any thought to possible alternative topics. How about a political biography of a former Labour leader? The idea appealed to me too. So I came to the meeting with two possible topics, both approved by the Head of Department.

The entire teaching staff was present at the meeting but Richard Brooker was not in the chair: he was stuck away in a corner and hardly acknowledged me. The Chairman introduced me to all eighteen present, identifying Alan Donaldson, who had been allocated to be my supervisor. Then he asked about my proposed field of study. I looked across to Brooker, expecting him to take the lead but he said nothing. I launched confidently into plan A: it was promptly shot down. Social Credit, New Zealand's third party, didn't merit serious academic examination. I caught Brooker's eye; he looked away. 'So,' said the Chairman, 'any other ideas?' This time I opened with a defensive gambit. 'Well, Professor Brooker suggested writing a political biography of Walter Nash.' No way, it was agreed: you couldn't possibly produce a political biography as a PhD thesis, which specifically required a theoretical basis. 'So what *is* this chap going to do?' asked the Chairman. Had we been in Manchester or Leeds, say, this chap would have replied: 'Well, I'll tell you what I'm going to do: go home. Thanks for nothing!' But we had just travelled thirteen thousand miles: going home was not an option. Then, almost discursively, my putative supervisor, asked, 'So what have you been doing with yourself over the last year then, Tom?' I told them about the MA thesis, explaining rather plaintively my interest in third parties, and then mentioned Sleaford Road. Robertson's eyes lit up. 'That's it, everybody: The Politics of Education! There's a PhD topic if ever I met one.' To a man they agreed. The Head of Department uttered not a word.

In the meantime Mo had taken a cab into town to meet her new Principal and had been shown round the school. Since she was starting halfway through the school year she wouldn't be teaching her subject French; she would be 'X' on the timetable, filling in

66

wherever, whenever and whatever the need. At least she never got to teach Metalwork or coach the Fourth Fifteen.

By the end of that week, then, we had a place to live, I had a viable topic and a supervisor and Mo had a job to start on the following Monday. We moved in on the Friday afternoon and Mo sent me round the corner to Kelburn village to get two fillets of cod and some emery boards. 'You f'om Engrand?' smiled a jovial Chinaman, 'No cod here!' I finished up with boneless moki, which turned out to be a lot better than it sounds. The chemist was waiting on a new shipment of emery boards. 'Will I call back on Tuesday?' I enquired. 'Yeah...Tuesday...in about two months. We're expecting another shipment about then.'

That first year in New Zealand turned out to be among the worst of my life. We were a long way from home, family and friends, and though Mo was happy at her school, especially when she had a proper timetable and was teaching French, I had nowhere to work and was struggling to get a hold on my research topic: after all, I knew nothing about it. I had one advantage however, without which it might have been impossible. There had been a bulky Royal Commission report on the administration of education only a year previously and it provided a full description of all the major bodies involved, so all I had to do was master all this detail. Moreover a PhD in Social Science is supposed to make some contribution to analytical theory, to construct a model. Now models in the natural and physical sciences are generally replicable, reliable and testable, whereas your political 'science' theories can't be replicated, aren't always reliable and can almost never be tested; everything in politics depends upon contingency. The political philosopher Karl Popper had been pretty clear on this, and he had spent time at the Victoria University of Wellington, so he should know. Here I was, alone in a small room in a far away country, trying to construct an abstract theory about the workings of an education system of which I was ignorant when I really believed that such theories were largely a waste of time. At one stage I thought I was beginning to lose my marbles and went to see the local doctor. He told me I was working too hard and to take two weeks off and get out more. Could I read, I asked? Yes, but not about work. I went to the nearby Botanical Gardens every day for two weeks and, under generally sunny skies amidst the exotic flora, I immersed myself in Jane Austen. I read all the major works; felt much better and never looked back. Jane Austen – better than pills!

Slowly things got better. First, relief was provided by a trip to Sydney. Stanley Walker, my Master's supervisor at Sheffield had arranged an oral examination – a viva – with a Professor at the University of Sydney, conveniently only 1,386 miles away. I had five very pleasant days in Sydney and came home with an MA (Econ). Back in windy Wellington David Donaldson, my supervisor introduced me to people in the Education Research Association and they found me temporary office space. I was able to talk to knowledgeable people about what I was doing on a daily basis. By the end of that first year I was increasingly confident that I knew what I had to do, and this transformed my world. In addition I had made friends at the Association, including a charming man with whom I began to play squash, and I resumed my rugby career at the University.

In 1960s New Zealand there was no obvious poverty or any signs of great affluence, and no hereditary social elite. Crime, apart from crimes of passion, was almost unheard of, and nobody went without. One Sunday Mrs. Mayfield's son-in-law was to take his family sailing but awoke to a flooded kitchen. Apologising for calling on a Sunday he explained his predicament to the plumber. Unfortunately the plumber couldn't help: he was taking the family sailing. Was this country 'Edwardian'? Largely; equal? Emphatically; dull? You'd better believe it!

Not long after we had arrived I'd found myself talking to a rather earnest middle-aged man at a party. He asked what I was doing in Wellington and how we were spending our leisure time. We'd been to the pictures several times. He sought my views on a 'B' film made by a New Zealand company, listened intently, and then added: 'I'm glad you liked my film (*his* film!). D'you know what, I think you could make a success in film. Here's my card. If you get pissed off any time, give me a call. And I really mean it!' In New Zealand if you were ambitious and prepared to work hard you could probably do whatever you wanted, within reason.

My first attempt at fieldwork was at a regional Education Board where I was to examine the pressures that shaped decision-making. The Chairman, from Shropshire, mentioned the 'Peroa Case'. Peroa was an industrial area in decline and its school role was falling; closure was under active consideration. The Catholic Bishop offered to share Peroa School and the Holy Name Society, a champion of Catholic education – and a constant nuisance to the government and the regional Boards – added its weight to the proposal. The Bishop had been misinformed: there was no spare capacity at the Peroa School, and in the meantime children were being bussed in from other state schools. Sounded interesting! The Chairman took me down to meet his CEO; a thick-set Kiwi with hard grey eyes. Having explained that I needed to look at the Peroa case, he left. The CEO asked me to explain all over again. His initial disdain morphed into loathing. Seizing me by the throat he rammed me back against the adjacent wall. 'You from the fuckin' Holy Name you bastard?' Self-defence was not one of the research skills I had acquired, but I managed to convince him I wasn't the enemy. We were to meet several times afterwards; he became almost civil. But I never did get to see that file.

The key word in my political lexicon had always been 'participation'. Let the people manage the things that affect them most, like schools. My research led to the discovery that most people couldn't give a monkey's and I concluded reluctantly that local participation was no guarantee of a fair or effective education system, or by extension political system. Popular participation, partisan politics, bureaucratic control: none of these suits modern government alone. A complex balance, *struck in public*, involving participants (parents), an independent, well-educated and liberal-minded bureaucracy and interested pressure groups is required; not easily constructed or maintained. But necessary.

In our second year in New Zealand I acquired a room to myself in the library building. Donaldson had discovered that an Economics PhD student, Grant Rae, had his own room up on the top floor: I would be able to share with him. I went up to break the good news to Grant, who seemed quite put out at the idea and had words with his tutor, a well-known mover-and-shaker. The upshot was that Grant maintained his independence but I too was moved-and-shaken into my own room next door. Grant and I became good friends. He would go on to a stellar career but even then he exuded dynamism.

Meanwhile I had met a young Canadian, also researching in 'Pol Sci'. Don and his wife Lizzi became our good friends. They introduced us to cosmopolitan life through the medium of spaghetti! Invited to dinner once we found ourselves confronted by two large dishes in the middle of the table, one containing what was later identified as spaghetti and the other a Bolognese sauce. Help yourselves said Lizzi. We sat bewildered. The only spaghetti we knew came in little orange tins and was eaten on toast but only *in extremis*. Lizzi patiently showed us how to serve the real thing. She deposited neat piles of pasta on our plates. You added sauce to taste. Simples! Mo couldn't wait to try it out on my neighbour Grant and his charming wife. They were just as mystified as we had been, so sticking my fork nonchalantly into the large pile of pasta in the middle of the table just as Lizzi had, I twirled it round – just as Lizzi had – and contrived to dump the whole lot onto the plate of an astonished Helen.

On a number of occasions my ignorance of academic procedures, deeper even than my ignorance of Italian pasta dishes, had nearly undone me, and now it was happening again. My scholarship was for three years, but it was assumed that I would apply for a year's extension to write up the research; apparently everybody did. Now, we had thought it would be best to get back to Britain in April, the start of the third school term, so that we could teach whilst looking for something more permanent. April 1968 would have been fine by us but nobody bothered to tell me about that extra year, so I went for April '67 and put myself under huge pressure to complete and submit my thesis and sit my viva to meet this self-imposed deadline.

The external examiner for my viva was a fellow Yorkshireman and things seemed to be going well when he casually remarked that the conceptual frame should be dropped (actually he used the word 'dumped'). Nonplussed, I asked about the required theoretical dimension. 'Yeah, but that's for a PhD,' he said. 'Isn't that what this is all about?' I asked, now well and truly rattled. 'Well I was talking about a potential book, not your bloody PhD. I've no problems with *that*.' Turning to Brooker the internal examiner, he went on: 'Didn't you tell him we liked it, Dick?' Brooker, flustered, said something about that being hardly proper. 'You straight-laced old bugger! Let's have the sherry out!' And so I became Doctor Tom.

Sad to leave now we had our feet under the table? Not really. We'd missed friends and families, missed the social and cultural vibrancy of Britain. We craved a more cosmopolitan lifestyle, pubs that were social institutions not places to get hammered. There was one pub in Wellington that allowed in unaccompanied women, the only one I knew with a carpet. One Friday just before closing when it was my shout and I was queuing along with half of Wellington with my arm-full of beer jugs, a man two places in front, unwilling to lose his place, peed on the carpet. Another feature of Wellington life we wouldn't miss was our fault line. One Sunday in the winter of 1966 we experienced a minor earthquake. We took tremors for granted but this time the whole house shook, the wood creaked and groaned and the hall ceiling undulated. From the bowels of the earth came a deep churning noise that neither of us wanted ever to hear again.

We had explored most of this arrestingly beautiful country from the bright art-deco city of Napier, Ninety-Mile Beach and the magical Bay of Islands in the north down south to Invercargill and that tiny village in Fjordland so remote it had no 'phones, only Morse code. The emptiness seemed to encourage hospitality and steely resilience amongst its people and a reasonably harmonious racial diversity. But it wasn't home.

Just before we left Alan Donaldson mentioned a position that was coming up in the Department; they wanted me to apply. I declined politely, pointing out that I really wasn't sure that I wanted to work in a university. Robertson's jaw dropped. 'What the hell else *are* you cut out for, Tom?' Had I heroically but inadvertently painted myself into a corner?

Ch.7: *Britannia's Embrace*

Some journey home! In those days the cost of air travel was prohibitive and the only way ordinary people could travel to the bottom of the world was by sea – a journey of over five weeks. Almost nobody went that far for a holiday: they mostly emigrated. The upcoming departure of each vessel for the Antipodes was recorded on the front page of *The Times* and as the ships sailed off families would knot together ropes of nylon stockings which would reach from ship to shore. As the ship pulled away the stocking would stretch as the band played *Now is the Hour*. Finally the stocking ropes would beak: those at either end might never see each other again. Same thing Down Under, though usually the travellers going north would return after a few years. We however had decided to fly north, stopping off in romantic places we had previously only dreamed about. To Hell with the cost.

Our first destination was Sydney, home now to Don and Lizzi. The shell of Utzon's revolutionary Opera House stood out impressively on the harbour skyline but we were more captivated by the delicate iron work on those terraces around King's Cross. From Sydney we flew up to Brisbane to stay with friends from Sheffield. They drove us into the rain forest and took us to see the Gold Coast, over-the-top even then, with its meter maids in their gold bikinis. We flew across the endless red deserts of the north, up over the Philippines to Hong Kong where we stayed in Kowloon overlooking the bustling Victoria Harbour. The sumptuous temples of Bangkok were even more exotic. Though the Vietnam War was being fought not far away, there was no

American military presence in Thailand, so it was odd that our hotel was full of young males with very short hair and odd names like 'Sarge' and 'Corp'. Being devoured by an Indian crowd at Delhi Airport was a harrowing experience. At our hotel, Claridges, we were bullied into having porridge for breakfast next morning by a majestic Sikh waiter. Porridge was the hallmark of the true Brit, he assured us. No porridge? Must be Australian! We took a taxi to the Taj Mahal with a monosyllabic Finn, passing through small towns brimming with poverty, squalor, cows, dogs, vehicles of all kinds from bicycles to bullock carts. Ambassador taxis nudged into the tightest places and exotically painted lorries did their best to follow. At the end of this nerve-jarring odyssey of heat, dust and confusion stood the Taj Mahal, the most serenely beautiful building in the world. The early morning flight from Delhi up towards the Mediterranean provided us with sunrise over the Himalayas at breakfast, better even than porridge.

The spectacular Roman temple complex at Baalbek was the highlight of Beirut. The lowlight was the unmistakable clawing in my gut that signified the advent of Delhi Belly. A high temperature and giddiness followed, persuading me to forgo the anticipated pleasures of Istanbul and Athens and take a flight through to London. Mo made an urgent call to my parents and in the evening of that same day, two years and seven months after we had left, our plane deposited us at Heathrow. This journey had been a spectacular finale to our great adventure. Some of the places we visited are now popular holiday destinations. For most people in the 'sixties they were the stuff of dreams. Surely we would be able to dine out on tales of the sites we had seen for the rest of our lives. Some hopes!

My parents managed to organise a homecoming party, and though I wasn't well placed to make the most of it, it was wonderful to see everyone again. And all pretty much as we'd left them. Now we had to make a life for ourselves back in Albion, though for several days more I was more engaged in my battle with Delhi Belly. That second week in April turned out to be the coldest week of the year. The skies were sullen and the wind biting; East London was utterly cheerless. By the time I was feeling somewhat better we took the train up to Lincolnshire to stay in Fulton with Henry and Doreen. Lincolnshire seemed forlorn, drab, and apologetic – and the people looked pinched. Returning to Fulton, Mo saw it now as if through my eyes on my first visit. She seemed to hold her parents personally responsible for living in a house that was small and poky and cold in country that was flat and featureless. She wanted to be back in New Zealand, or anywhere but Lincolnshire. But I had other plans. A telegram to Peterborough Education Office on the day after our return produced an invitation to have a chat with one of the officers. We were to go over next day in our newly acquired car.

Towards the end of our time in Wellington I had written to ask Henry to keep an eye open for a VW Beetle and purchase it on our behalf. Never in a million years, said Mo, would Henry buy a car for someone without their seeing it first. By return of post came the news that Henry had bought a pale blue 1963 Beetle for £350. Four days later came another letter: he had bought another one, grey this time. Mo fell over. We could choose which one we preferred; he would be happy to have the other. We chose the blue.

At the Education Offices we didn't see either of the officers that I knew, but I felt it safe to assume that the man who spoke to us would be aware of my history. I made it clear that we would be unable firmly to commit ourselves beyond that summer term. Moreover it was essential that jobs be found for both of us. Go and get something to eat, said the officer; come back at 2pm when he would be in a position to let us know how things stood. Back at the office we discovered that the Authority had a place for Mo but not me. This wasn't what was supposed to happen! *Please* come back to us, they had said – *anytime*. We had to thank the officer and politely decline. Then, off the cuff, I suggested we drive straight on to King's Lynn and present ourselves to the Education Office there. By 4pm or thereabouts we had both been signed up to teach in single-sex secondary schools separated by about half a mile. Moreover, we were given an introduction to a local solicitor who had a small property on his books that might be suitable for us to rent. This was Thursday; we were to start the following Monday, first full week of the new term. On Sunday we moved into our new abode and on Monday morning, we took a deep breath, conjured up a whistle, and set off on our different ways.

Later that day we received a monster telegram from Peterborough Education Office, offering us both jobs. Mo's sounded a good job but mine was amazing: a supernumerary head of department's post at one of the best grammar schools in the area. As a supernumerary I could do as much or as little teaching as I chose and be paid at Head of Department rate. A promising career was on offer here. A council house in a relatively pleasant part of town was also on offer. So they *had* remembered me... too late! I wrote back regretfully declining.

Mo's job turned out to be the pits. King's Lynn is a fine mediaeval port but the behaviour of the daughters of the waterside at Dashwood Park Secondary School for Girls was devoid of olde worlde charm but full of dockside coarseness. On the whole Mo found her charges foul-mouthed and totally uninterested in learning French. Before we had left for the Antipodes drug abuse by the young was pretty much unheard of: it didn't even feature in my teacher-training course. Now drugs were common amongst young people and teachers had to learn how to deal with the problems. Well, Mo didn't know how and neither, it seemed, did any of her middle-aged, small-minded colleagues. Mo became inured to the girls' behaviour after a time but never grew to like them, and she received no support or flicker of friendship from the staff. Perhaps they had been in the front line too long. Most days she would come home at the end of the afternoon and cry.

To make matters worse I had fallen on my feet. The Alderman Cartledge Secondary School for Boys was not in the vanguard of scholarship. Most of the boys came in from the Norfolk countryside, including the Sandringham Royal Estate, but on the whole they were as good as gold. A senior teacher introduced me to the classes I was to teach. In one his eye fell on a large raw-boned young man. 'Ah, Borthwick,' he said in that soft Norfolk burr. 'Stand up so's Mr. Spring here can have a look at you, boy. Now Mr. Spring, this here's Borthwick, and Borthwick, well, he got a problem. (Stage whisper) He have to pee a lot, don't you boy?' Borthwick smiled complicitly. 'If Borthwick put his hand up and say he want a pee, you let him go Mr. Spring. If you was to say him: "No boy, you only just bin," he'd prob'ly pee on the floor. Don't mean nothing by it, mind. That's just the way it is.'

Borthwick's incontinence turned out to be about the worst problem I was to encounter teaching in Norfolk.

As the term wore on, two jobs in the university world in the field of Politics were advertised, one was at the Bournemouth College of Advanced Technology and the other at the University of Hull. I decided to apply for both. I was invited to interview at Bournemouth. Nice place, balmy, almost continental. It might prove difficult for Mo to find a position, but one step at a time. The interview was hard going. The Head of Economics, who would be my boss, was singularly unimpressed that, given the choice, I had decided to study as an undergraduate at Sheffield instead of Manchester, which was well-known to be far and away the best provincial Politics Department in the country. I fancy he wouldn't have been won over had I explained that my choice was based upon the fact that Manchester wasn't in Yorkshire. We three applicants went out together for lunch. One was a young, sharply dressed Nigerian with a cut-glass Oxford English accent, the other a somewhat older man from Cambridge in a brown three-piece suit with a floppy silk handkerchief hanging from the breast pocket. When we returned I was called in. The chairman, the Head of Economics who had seemed so hostile earlier, offered me the job: my starting salary would be £2,300 and added: 'What a young man would find to spend that much on I don't know – but those are my instructions,' I would be teaching Politics on the external degree course of the University of London, would be getting a handsome salary and living in a very pleasant environment. I said yes.

I got home the next day to a letter from the University of Hull inviting me for interview the following week. We had a long chat about the propriety of going for a job having already accepted another. We agreed: the institution concerned, though inconvenienced, would appoint the candidate ranked second, as presumably they would have done had I been run over on the way home. For the individual – me in this case – it was their career, their life. I would go to Hull. I'd been there only once to play rugby. When we came out onto the field, the wind – straight from the Steppes – was like nothing I'd met before: penetratingly sharp and carrying the smell of dead fish. And we got thoroughly worked over. I thought that if I never saw Hull again that would be soon enough. And now I was applying for a job there. When we told the Olivers that I was intending to motor up to Yorkshire for the interview Henry surprisingly said he would like to come. It turned out to be a long journey on a hot June afternoon up an A17, the spine of Lincolnshire, clogged with lorries, to Scunthorpe, then on through the desolate marshes to Goole and finally along the north bank of the Humber to Hull. Rooms had been booked for us in a hotel in town.

The following morning we went out hunting for the University. We had a map but still managed to get halfway to Beverley before realising we'd missed our turn. Several locals were interrogated but only the last knew that Hull actually had a university, never mind where it was. However, he was able to put us right and we duly turned up half an hour before the interview. Perfect. I suggested that Henry might like to go for a walk and get a coffee because I didn't foresee having my business done for about an hour and a half. But he wasn't listening; he'd been unhappy about an engine noise and needed to explore. Suddenly, in my sports jacket and flannels, I found myself holding a greasy carburettor while Henry tinkered with a spanner. What was happening here?

I explained I had to be off, but Henry wasn't listening. He went to hand me another lump of engine. With less than ten minutes to go I thrust the carburettor and engine lump into his hands and shot off. I headed for the cloakroom to wash the grease off my hands. No hot water! I did my best. Five minutes to go. I got directions to the interview room, and as I charged up the stairs a plaque in bronze set into the wall caught my eye: it held a quotation from Winston Churchill extolling the virtues of university education. What did he know? Nevertheless at that moment *I* knew that this was what I wanted to do for the foreseeable and this was where I wanted to do it. Sweaty, breathless and with oily hands I arrived with about a minute to spare and found myself ushered in immediately.

The interview went well. After all I was coming with two successful research theses behind me and two published journal articles. The Vice Chancellor offered me the job on the spot, explaining that they were keen to have me, and to prove the point they would forego the normal first level of appointment as Assistant Lecturer and put me two points up the full Lecturers' scale. They were offering me £1,700: who could refuse? I shook the Vice Chancellor's hand with my somewhat oily one. On the way out I saw amongst the other candidates the young Nigerian from Bournemouth, whose mouth dropped open. 'But…I thought…you'd taken Bournemouth,' he stammered. I opened my hands in a silent gesture intimating; 'I know; life's a bugger.' When I got back to the car the engine was all back in one piece and Henry was reading a newspaper. On the way home we stopped in a pub for fish and chips and a beer. Later I dropped Henry off in Fulton and went on to King's Lynn to break the news to Mo. At least it would be easier for her to find a job in Hull! My mum was surprised to hear about my change of heart, but guessed I knew what I was doing. I ended our conversation as I had an earlier one with Mo. 'Still, it'll only be for two or three years.' I was confident that I wouldn't find myself regretting this decision the way I had Bournemouth. As it happened, a few weeks later I received a charming letter from the Head of Politics at Bristol University, who, as an external examiner, had read my undergraduate dissertation four years earlier. He was encouraging me to apply for a post there. Sounded nice, Bristol, but I couldn't face the prospect of meeting that young gentleman from Nigeria again.

Four weeks till the end of term: four weeks of purgatory for Mo and four weeks of easy-paced entertaining with a little bit of History for me. Life for both of us outside school was pleasant enough. We spent a good deal of time motoring round north Norfolk visiting mediaeval churches, priories and castles, and exploring the coast. One weekend in early July Butch Harris, now a married man, organised a welcome-home party for us. He had a large flat in Northampton and nearby, by chance, lived Andy Lynch, who was also married. All our mates turned up except Gareth and his new wife, who were teaching in Canada. Kieran and Philip came with spouses. Nathan came alone.

Kieran had married a red-haired PE teacher of Glaswegian stock, whom we took to immediately. He was not only married but a father – of *two* sons, separated by only eleven months. Despite his enhanced status as a parent Kieran's mastery of life skills was as tenuous as ever. Kirsty his wife told us that the previous Saturday they were to go out for the evening and had arranged for her sister to babysit. Whilst Kirsty was upstairs

, a spruced up Kieran had been in charge of the boys. ished yell from below brought her rushing out of the ı to discover mayhem. Moments earlier Kieran had ha, ined to glance up briefly from his *Guardian* to find himself confronted by two poo-covered children and one partly poo-covered wall – and on his watch! He did the only thing a sensitive father could: threw up over the carpet. His had been the cry of anguish. Good job Glaswegians are tough. These occasional traumas notwithstanding, they seemed very much at ease with each other. Philip, too, had married. His wife had been married previously, unhappily. Though in the early years of marriage they had severe cash flow problems and Anna was virtually penniless, she came from a family with promising business contacts. When we met Anna I could understand what had drawn Philip to her: she was vivacious, dynamic and focused, and she was clearly going places. Philip had met his mate.

We had to acquire a place to live in Hull before the start of the university term in October, but there was still time for a short holiday and Kieran suggested that the four of us go camping. That week in Devon was hardly memorable: it never stopped raining. Things were so bad one afternoon that we went into Ilfracombe and watched *Carry on Camping*. We swam a good deal, once during a hailstorm. At the end of the week we headed straight back to Norfolk. Before leaving for the north we spent a few days in Fulton. Doreen asked me to dig over her garden since gardening wasn't Henry's thing. She was particularly concerned about a burgeoning mass of horseradish. It couldn't be eradicated, she warned, only contained. All next day I dug until I was waist-deep, and I *did* eradicate the horseradish, permanently; that part of

Lincolnshire would never be the same again. *Si monumentum requiris, circumspice...* Now for Yorkshire.

In 1293 Edward I acquired the small riverside town of Wyke, made it into a port to supply his armies in Scotland and gave his new port a royal charter. Nestling along the northern bank of the Humber, the city of Hull is divided east/west by the River Hull, a tributary of the Humber: hence the city's Sunday name, Kingston-upon-Hull. Proximity to the Low Countries gave Kingston a strategic importance; decisively, during the English Civil War the city prevented King Charles from restocking his war machine from his nearby fleet. Hull went on to become one of Britain's major fishing ports with a strong interest in whaling. Later it suffered as the most bombed British city in the Second World War per head of population. Though the city centre, rebuilt in the 1950s after the air raids is dispiritingly bland, Hull has its comfortable suburbs, a mediaeval quarter and a very pleasant Victorian/Edwardian enclave, which later become a conservation area known locally as The Avenues. The University, on a leafy campus, is traditional redbrick, founded in 1927 and awarded its charter in 1954. Nobody outside of the East Riding knows any of this, or indeed anything else about Hull except that it later acquired a famous bridge as a result of an infamous by-election pledge. Years later I was recruiting students for Hull University in Germany, and told my audience that Hull had the longest suspension bridge in the world. 'Yes, we have heard,' said one young man. 'The bridge from nowhere to nowhere.' This seemed to be how Hull was generally perceived. But it had its charms. It might have been described by one or two rugby league supporters on their visits from the West Riding as the backside of Yorkshire, but it was undeniably Yorkshire, and proud of it. To our surprise, we rather took to Hull.

One of my new colleagues told us of a first-floor flat in a large Edwardian house in The Avenues that was for rent. The owner wanted £7 per week, which if not cheap was hardly a deal breaker: it was rather elegant and we took it. Not only did we have a place to stay but Mo had been offered a job in a secondary school in East Hull. Though nothing special, Eastlands was a relief after King's Lynn. Six months had passed now since our return from exile and in that time we had reacquainted ourselves with England. I found my homeland a revelation: I fell in love with its subtly coloured landscapes; its architectural and topographical variety; its rich regional culture and accents, the quiet consideration of most of its people, and perhaps most of all the sense of history that underpinned everything. I was glad to be home, gladder still to be living once again in the county of my birth. And we had seen so much of the world that we wouldn't need to travel again – ever!

Ch.8: *Stick or Twist?*

'So when you gonna get a *real* job, Tom?' one of my Cockney cousins asked. Fair question: where I came from a job meant producing something tangible, something that 'society' needed. For nearly all the adults I had known as a child that meant physical work. Society also needed workers-by-brain, like doctors, managers, lawyers, and school teachers and so on, we knew that, but working *in a university*? I'd had to explain to my mum and dad what every step on my academic progress meant – just after I'd got the hang of it myself. Like me they didn't understand about undergraduate degrees, still less about postgraduate degrees and as for being a doctor – one whose job *wasn't* to take tonsils out – well, what was that all about? There was social kudos to be gained in those days for working-class parents, especially in somewhere like the Isle of Dogs, from having a child up at university, but you can overdo these things. I'd been 'up at university' since 1959! I should be out working – and having a family: James and Nicky had two children now. I couldn't quite excise the feeling that my cousin was dead right: in my heart I also believed that the career I was embarking on had only tenuous connections to the real world. Maybe, *maybe*, I could still fulfil my earlier vague ambition and escape into politics – when I'd established a name for myself. But in the meantime, an academic life? For me?

I came to Hull with some problems. I'd completed my research, got my thesis typed up, submitted and examined and all within two and a half years. I'd actually *returned* money to the Scholarship Fund! I met no-one who had equalled this record or indeed anyone daft enough to aspire to (though I believe that

Robert Mugabe's wife completed her PhD in five months. Children, don't try this at home!) And all because nobody told me how the system worked. Well, I was to suffer for it. For the first couple of years at Hull I felt that I was walking a tightrope. At concerts I would have to battle against the urge to stand and just shout. I suffered with hypochondria, slept badly and sometimes had vivid dreams. One night I dreamt that Mo and I had been bound tight to a railway track – no doubt by a villain in black with a thin waxed moustache – and a train was approaching. I had to break out of those ropes by sheer physical power and haul Mo to safety. I failed, though I did manage to save the bedclothes. I found myself on the floor in the far corner of the room protectively embracing the blankets, and there was Mo sitting upright in bed wondering what the hell was going off. We laughed it away but I knew it was a sign of a struggle to retain my sanity, a struggle I waged in secret and on my own.

Added to my existential problem was a deeper-seated one; I knew more than enough academics to doubt whether I was one. When I arrived in Hull, I was one of four new members of the Politics Department in that year. There was a graduate of King's College who was in the throes of completing his PhD. He had been appointed as an Assistant Lecturer. There was a Hungarian who had fled his homeland in the 1956 revolution. He was several years older than me and came with a wife and young family. Finally there was an avuncular Aberdonian who had come to a Senior Lectureship. They were very different in terms of personality and aspiration but had something in common: each was confident in and wedded to his field of expertise. I would never have described myself as a scholar at this time and still saw myself as a man of action awaiting the call.

The Politics Department was housed in two inter-war semis on the edge of the campus. I had a rather poky upstairs room to myself. Two shared a larger room next door to me, Paul Johnson the King's man and Owen, who had come the year before. Owen was a bit deaf and compensated by speaking loudly; he was known affectionately as The Honk. I shared the tutorial teaching with him on the course for which I provided the lectures, *An Introduction to British Politics*. There have been a number of MPs in the House of Commons who were introduced to British politics on that course.

There were ten in the Politics Department all told including the Head. Ralph Alders reminded me of a dentist: intense, thin-faced, rimless glasses, short on words. He had a habit of stroking his forehead when speaking. As a lad he had been involved in a cycling accident, fracturing his skull. When the weather was muggy he would suffer agonies from headaches. Raif was a Londoner by birth and disposition, and looked upon his time in Yorkshire as extended community service. The only one in the Department other than me who wondered what on earth he was doing there was the son of a Derby bookmaker. I mistook his initial kindnesses for tokens of friendship; it wasn't his fault he didn't like me. On the other hand he offered me some life-saving advice: whenever you doubt your fitness to be teaching in a university, he said, go over to the staff common room and listen in on the conversations. You'll soon discover you're one of only a few in the whole room with any common sense. (Actually he was a bit more forthright.) It worked! The others at Hull were bright, self-absorbed academics a few of whom seemed to want to make it their business to know your business and preferably before you did. All this did little to reassure a young man who would have doubted his mission even in the most hospitable and easy-going company.

Amongst my new colleagues I found most in common with Robert Nagy the Hungarian, who was a political philosopher. We began to go out for a couple of beers from time to time. Nagy could give the impression of being – well in fact he often was – your typically taciturn central European. He was also a soccer fanatic, and persuaded me to accompany him to Boothferry Park to watch Hull City. At the time Hull City had not long secured promotion from the old Third Division North to the Second. I enjoyed the games but was never able to persuade Bob to come with me to the Boulevard to watch the rugby league, which was becoming my own focus of interest.

Bob's history set him apart from your average academic. He came from Budapest where he played the drums in a rock band. In 1956 he decided to get out of Hungary with his young wife and her daughter from a previous marriage, to whom Anna had given birth when she was sixteen, and they endured a nerve-wracking escape into Austria. Slowly they made their way to London where Bob, without a word of English, got a job as a porter at Harrods. He and Anna lodged with an older workmate and his wife, who had befriended them. This friendship gave them not only a sense of stability but, on their deaths later these friends left Bob and Anna a small fortune.

Having acquired a command of English Bob began studying A Levels in the evenings. On the strength of two 'A's in Politics and Economics he secured a place at LSE where he subsequently graduated with a First Class Honours degree and won a scholarship to Cambridge for a PhD. Ten years after arriving in London with no English Robert Nagy had become a lecturer in Politics at a British university. Kind of knocked my little achievements into a cocked hat. Bob recognises me as a fellow proletarian, and we became and remained firm friends.

Alastair Duncan the Aberdonian – Uncle Alastair as the students called him – looked like a farmer with his checked shirts, tweed jacket, straw-coloured hair, rosy cheeks, bushy eyebrows and pipe. He had a penchant for Edwardian phrases, like 'sticky dog' for when things weren't going too well; a phrase that was to come in handy when he subsequently took over as acting Head of Department for a year.

My first full year at Hull proved an eventful one. 1968 was the year of revolution when student radicalism emerged all over the Western world. In East Yorkshire 'Spot' Fanshaw briefly became almost a public figure. One morning at the beginning of an examination Spot stood up, tore up his exam paper symbolically and shouted 'down with indoctrination' and left the hall. By happy coincidence the cameras of Anglia and Yorkshire TV were waiting outside, and he tore up another exam paper equally spontaneously and gave an interview to waiting reporters. The Students' Union occupied the administration block and declared an official sit-in. In London in spring a peaceful march to the American Embassy, which was supposed to culminate in Vanessa Redgrave delivering an anti-Vietnam War petition, ended in a massive riot, with hundreds of arrests. In Paris the students were marching with the workers against the regime of Charles de Gaulle. In the USA students were marching against the Vietnam

War – in fact two years later four were shot dead in Ohio at Kent State University. In Hull the objectives of the revolution were more focused: three questions instead of four in Finals Examination papers, and student representatives at departmental meetings.

Raif Alders was off in New York for the year and Alastair had taken over. Alastair offered no firm leadership, but that really wasn't such a bad strategy: although it earned a reputation for radicalism the Department survived intact. For the next three years or so 'revolution' hung in the air in Hull like the threat of unpleasant drizzle. So what, after all, did they gain, these Yorkshire Toussaints and Luxemburgs? They got their three questions and not four in Finals papers! Students' interests began to be taken account of in a way that hadn't happened before, and students were given places on university governing bodies as well as having the right to be represented in departmental meetings. Henceforth boredom and ineffectuality would be shared more democratically.

In the second term of that first year Mo began a new job. She had got a position in a girl's High School just a few streets away. This made life so much easier from a travel point of view and so much more rewarding from a teaching one. At least it would have done had she not chosen to slip over in the playground at the end of her very first day and crack her ankle. It turned out to be a Potts Fracture and required pinning, so Mo spent several days in the Infirmary and several months convalescing, mostly on the sofa. At home in Lincolnshire, Mo had always had cats around her. It occurred to me that the acquisition of a house-trained moggy would buck her up. So late one Friday afternoon in February I drove to a small pet shop on the Anlaby Road and for five shillings acquired a small but continent black kitten which, just like my mice all those years ago, was neatly wrapped up in a large brown paper bag. That's how I brought it home. As usual, Mo was on the sofa reading the paper. I tossed the bag on her lap. She mumbled something but took no notice until it began to move. She dropped the *Guardian* and just as she was about to examine the bag a little black head popped out. We called him Winkle and he proved a great acquisition, especially over the next few months.

At the end of our first year in Hull we moved to a larger, cheaper but less well appointed flat, owned by the University, and began to acquire some furniture. Towards the end of that first term in 1968 we got a message from Australia: Don and Lizzi were going home to Canada and on the way planned to spend six months or so in Britain. They would buy a car and drive around the country but would need a base – could they stay with us? They expected to arrive in early April. Before then a long cold winter had to be endured. There was no central heating in the new flat and our main defence against the cold was the installation of a Dutch psychologist in the flat below, who didn't like the damp Yorkshire winters. He and his delightful Indonesian wife, who liked them even less, would maintain a huge coal fire every day and we got the benefit. He was an intoxicating character; the only continental I knew who understood cricket.

He bought a Corgi! What's a right-on psychologist doing with a Corgi? And the hound had to be trained. Naturally Anders knew his Pavlov: he would roll up a newspaper of an evening and smacked it against his thigh, then throw the dog out into the garden until it did a jobby. He did this every day after dinner, reasoning that soon the hound would associate the whack of paper

93

on thigh with having a poo in the garden. I saw Anders a few weeks later and asked how the master-plan was working. 'Oh just great,' he said. 'Every time I sit down to read *The Guardian* after dinner that fucking dog sits in front of my chair and craps on the carpet.' So what was he doing about it? Well, he was at a loss, he admitted. On three occasions he'd walked the dog, taking a different circuitous route each time, over to the far side of Pearson Park, thrown it a stick and when the dog ran after it Anders bolted home the quick way. Each time when he got back home there was the Corgi waiting. After a few months he handed it on, only too grateful to be rid: I bet the feeling was mutual.

Early in the new academic year, with the prospect of house ownership before us, we began to think about furniture. Mo drew my attention to a newspaper article that extolled the virtues of Victorian pine furniture. Usually painted brown or green these pieces could be bought for just a few pounds. Underneath the nondescript paint, however, was often a honey-coloured gem. How could you tell? Take a thre'penny Joey with you and give it a little scrape. If it was pine, you should buy it, take it home and strip it with paint remover, and when pristine, wax it or give it a coat of clear varnish. A nice antique piece for about a fiver! This inaugurated a fashion that swept the British professional classes. We went for a walk down Spring Bank and immediately bought two wall cupboards for £5 the pair and set to work. They turned out to be Georgian and when finished looked like reasonable quality furniture. We bought six pieces in all, some large, and I began to clean them using paint remover and then brushing on a coat of a new alternative to varnish, polyurethane. What I didn't know was that these 'polys' gave off fumes to which I was allergic: I was poisoning myself.

It was at Easter of 1969 that Don and Lizzi arrived and by then my lack of energy was leading to lack of appetite and most significantly to an increasing lack of weight. A variety of tests proved negative so as far as the medical profession was concerned I was alright. Not unreasonably I took a different view; after all by now I had lost more than a stone and could hardly climb stairs. Convinced I was on the way out I thought that there were two things I could do to help my widow-to-be: to teach her to drive and to finish off the work on the furniture. So I took her out driving in the East Riding as often as possible and redoubled my cleaning and varnishing – and got worse more rapidly. Things had got so bad by summer that I couldn't manage to stay up to watch the moon landing on July 20th. I went to bed and asked to be wakened when the Eagle was landing. On the plus side Mo was now a competent driver and passed her test at the second attempt. Moreover I finished the furniture. Mo could manage without me now! Mysteriously, though, as summer progressed, I slowly began to get better.

Now we could give serious attention to finding a house. The University provided an interest-free loan of half of the deposit, a generous gesture. Since we'd expect to pay about £4,000 for a standard semi-detached house, and the deposit would be 10 per cent, that meant we needed only to save something over £200 to be serious contenders in the house market. Well, we'd actually saved that by the previous Christmas but one Friday I bought a turntable, amplifier and speakers from Comet for just under £200. Mo was speechless, but forgave me the first time she heard *The Swan of Tuonela* in high fidelity.

After some searching we settled on a semi-detached house in Willerby, to the west of Hull. Don and Lizzi were still around to help us with the move. I was delighted to be able to help carry the furniture and the four of us soon had the place in good shape. There was one job to be done, taking out a large built-in kitchen cabinet; useful but ugly. Just on the off-chance I scratched it with a Joey: underneath it was a lovely honey-coloured pine. Out came the paint stripper and I made a start; that was when I began to feel the lethargy, breathlessness and dizziness stirring. So this was the secret of my earlier illness! What to do? Don and Lizzi stripped the unit for us and it looked great.

When we left for New Zealand back in 1964 we missed the election of Labour leader Harold Wilson and failed to benefit from the white heat of Labour's technological revolution. Two years later Wilson went to the people and obtained a good working majority: now to build the New Jerusalem! This was what I had been waiting for since 1959. Almost immediately the country was plunged into a damaging seamen's strike and the currency was devalued. What is it they say about being careful what you wish for? Labour didn't modernise the economy or the social structure but these *were* years of revolutionary cultural change. This was the Age of Aquarius, of free love, of Woodstock. No doubt this had all been fermenting for some time but not in Wellington it hadn't. Back home, in the summer of 1969 we went to see Ken Russell's new film *Women in Love* in which not only did Oliver Reed and Alan Bates wrestle naked in front of an open fire, but Glenda Jackson whipped off her nightdress. That act, for which three years in 'Edwardian' Wellington left us totally unprepared, brought the temple of traditional British restraint crashing down on us. We came out of the cinema shell-shocked. After all, we weren't the baby-boomers, the children of the '60s; our revolutionary settlement hadn't included famous actresses flashing their bristols in your face. Sex, drugs and rock and roll: famously it all came too late for Hull's lugubrious librarian Philip Larkin – and for us too – but least he'd seen them coming.

Hard times, these, for me: I was apprehensive about my choice of careers, worried about my health, and just generally pissed off. I didn't like the shape of the country's politics or the direction that Britain's cultural values seemed to be taking, though as an 'intellectual' I suppose I should have been in the vanguard of change. And above all, where *was* that political opening?

Ch.9: *Staking a Claim*

Lashings of cold rain that first autumn in our new house but we didn't care: by late summer it had become clear that Mrs. Maureen Spring was going to become a mother. This was a game-changer. We would now be staying put in the East Riding and I working at the University of Hull for the foreseeable. We knew nothing about pregnancy and so, having no easy access to family wisdom, began to read up on it. One thing we learned was that you weren't 'safely' pregnant until you had passed the first three months, and we were devastated when, at the end of October Mo began to bleed and took to her bed. A rather haughty doctor made it clear that this was no big deal, but for Mo and me it was a very big deal. For three long days this deal of contestable dimension hung in the balance. The viability of the embryo had been a subject of public debate a few years earlier during the framing of the 1967 Abortion Law reforms. Probably we stood somewhere between the position later championed by Monty Python's Yorkshireman – every sperm is sacred – and the position ascribed to modern Jewish metropolitan culture that the embryo isn't truly viable until it has graduated from Law School. Finally we lost the baby. Ah, but was it a baby after only three months? Well it was for us. Matters were made worse by the fact that only two doors away Paul Johnson's wife Emma had safely cleared the three month hurdle and was beginning to bloom. Paul was already busy painting and installing his child's first set of book shelves.

Meanwhile autumn had given way to winter and the icy East Riding wind only deepened our already low spirits, and now we had no freezing Dutchman to warm the house up for us. We invested in a large second-hand paraffin stove and placed it next to the stairs in the hall, calling it our 'oil-fired central heating'. It helped. That winter I used to cycle the five miles to the University, frequently through snow and on one bitterly cold morning my eyebrows and newly acquired beard froze up. My bike was unique. I had bought it for £6 at a second-hand shop that specialised in things that looked OK but didn't work properly; my bike fitted the bill exactly. There was a ball-bearing missing from the chainset so the turning circle incorporated a noticeable lurch to the left which required deft management. There was a consolation however: bicycle theft was one of Hull's growth industries but nobody stole my bike, even though some evenings I found it twenty yards or so from where I'd left it.

Into that drear winter however came a shaft of sunshine: Mo discovered that she was pregnant again and though we spent the next few months on tenterhooks this time she had no problems at the twelve-week mark. We began to contemplate the summer with more confidence. Mo's steady expansion wasn't the only excitement of the summer of 1970: there was a General Election in June and Harold Wilson's hapless government was replaced by Edward Heath's Tories, who seemed determined to prove that hapless wasn't such a bad thing. Robert Peel was said to have had a smile like the silver plate on a coffin and much the same could be said about Heath. Never popular, he came to power, if truth be told, largely because of the public disenchantment, south of the border anyway, following England's 2-3 loss to Germany in the World Cup quarter-final, after they had been coasting at 2-0. Somebody had to suffer for this – why not Wilson? Things were getting worse nationally and globally, so it was good to have something positive to look forward to ourselves.

When the holidays came the ever-expanding Mo stopped teaching and began to enjoy a life of well-earned leisure. Meanwhile a potentially serious gynaecological problem was drawn to our attention: our blood groups were incompatible: I was B positive and Mo A negative. Rhesus negativity wasn't an issue to which either of us had given any thought. The advice was that there should be no problem with a first child but that we should think seriously about having any more because the baby might be at risk. Almost unbelievably however, as Mo got towards the end of her term, there was a medical breakthrough: providing the mother had an immunoglobulin injection immediately after giving birth there should be no danger to a subsequent child. Accordingly Mo approached the whole business of giving birth with greater confidence.

On the morning of July 9th she exchanged this confidence for mild panic as her birth pains began. I drove her to the Woodgates Maternity Home where she was booked in. In these days 'modern' men were being encouraged to stay for the birth: was I a modern man? When we arrived at the maternity home a formidable Scottish matron took Mo off my hands, fixed me with an unchallengeable Caledonian gaze and said: 'You'll be wanting away now young man; Maureen will be quite safe with us. We have your telephone number and will let you know as soon as anything happens.': clearly she wasn't a modern matron. Ten minutes later I had driven up onto the Wolds, parked the car and walked to a hill looking out over the Humber. I gazed down over the river, quietly contemplating the arrival of a Yorkshire person of our own. I said a little prayer. Slowly the light mist that had hung over the river started to lift and the sun began to dapple the

101

patchwork of what Larkin referred to as 'fields too thistle to be called meadows'. It was sometime before 7.30am and I was at peace with the world: but then, I didn't know what was coming.

It proved to be a long and stressful weekend. Mo was in labour all day Friday. Into Saturday and still nothing happened. I wasn't alarmed; perhaps if I had been better informed I would have been. In Lincolnshire lips were steadfastly pursed; on the Isle of Dogs my mum was having a bad time. Her sister Alice had been in labour for over fifty hours with her first child and it had been stillborn; fortunately mum had said nothing to me about this. On Sunday morning I was told that Mo had been moved to Beverley, the major maternity facility in the East Riding, where she would undergo a Caesarean section sometime after lunch. Every unforgiving minute of that sunny Sunday morning seemed filled with at least sixty seconds' worth of distance crawled. Then, sometime after 2pm the phone rang. I was upstairs washing. Anxious to get to the phone before my heart exploded I managed to lose my footing and crashed down the stairs on my backside, one at a time, grazing an arm, twisting a knee and bruising an elbow. It was Beverley: just after 2pm on Sunday October 11th Maureen Spring had given birth to a boy, Joshua Daniel Paul – Josh – who weighed in at 10lb 11 oz: mother and baby were fine. At that moment there was no happier man in the universe: a son of York! I phoned 12 Cawdor Street and when I heard my mother's voice I was unable to speak. My message was transmitted by grunts and gurgles but my mum seemed to understand; in no time the whole of the clan had the news. Next I phoned Henry and Doreen whose joy if more measured was palpable. An hour later, scrubbed up, smartly dressed, I was holding my son in my arms. I hadn't dared even imagine what this might feel like but just then I knew instinctively that this was what I had been brought into this world for: to do my best for this little man with big fists and any others that might follow him, for as long as I was needed. The little man himself might bring his parents much pleasure later in life – who knows? – but not much could surpass this moment.

The nurses thought him beautifully behaved, and considered that with hands like his he would become a great rugby league player. His father, on the other hand, saw him sporting a blue cap with a white rose. That's why he had three initials, in case he should open the Yorkshire batting. In fact he was to exhibit no special aptitude for sport as he grew up. Josh and Mo came home a week later. The day before, I had gone down to Lincolnshire to pick Doreen and Henry up so that they could see their new grandson and give Mo support.

By the time I took Doreen and Henry back Mo was more confident and in fact somewhat relieved to have her parents out of her hair. Josh continued to sleep soundly and the autumnal weather was just as well-behaved, so he spent most days sleeping outside in the pram. And from the start he was no fan of tight bedding; he would throw off the blankets almost as soon as he was cocooned. Being such a large lad Mo had trouble providing enough milk so, after rigorous training, I was called into action as a bottle-wallah. I liked that and Josh didn't seem to mind. As time wore on I discovered that I *was*, in many respects, quite a modern man.

Autumn became winter, winter gave way to spring and we'd hardly noticed: we became very comfortable with our son. It was about this time that Mo decided she would like another child. I hadn't imagined that we would be trying again for a couple of years but was happy to be persuaded. And with us to try was to succeed; by October of 1971 Mo had navigated the twelve week rapids and was sailing along fairly serenely. The fact that Josh caused so few problems had persuaded Mo that she could easily handle another child and Josh seemed to be able to manage his parents with ease; no doubt he could handle a sibling.

This time Mo went straight to Beverley and her labour was less traumatic. At 8lb 7oz the delivery of child number two, a young man named Timothy James Thomas Spring –Tim – was not an especially difficult, though he refused to come into the world without the aid of forceps. Uninvited to attend the birth by the nursing staff, I drove in to see my wife and our new son on Tuesday April 13th 1972, a glorious spring afternoon. I took one look at our new boy and actually jumped: 'That's my dad!' I stared down at Tim's dark Celtic features, so strong was the contrast to his brother's Nordic complexion and blonde hair. They were to grow more alike later but at the birth the difference was striking. My cup overflowed.

Back in Willerby the fort was being held by my mum who had come up just before Tim's birth. Tim turned out to be normal and woke every four hours for a feed so Mo was more frayed than last time, and my mum's support proved invaluable. Her ideas of a well-run household were considerably more regimented than ours, so the help came at a price and we were both grateful but relieved when she went back to the East End. Nevertheless it wasn't so easy to get into a routine. Doing the 2am milk shift I would get only a couple of hours sleep because Josh tended to waken at about five when he would entertain himself – and me – with extended extracts from the Ring Cycle sung in what sounded like Mandarin. I would go off to work feeling like a zombie. I had been teaching an A Level evening class down at the College of Commerce for a few years, to make a bit more money, and one evening not long after Tim's birth I fell asleep in the middle of a class leaning against a wall. Well, I wasn't the first; apparently Anthony Trollope frequently did the same thing and he didn't have the excuse of teaching A Level British Constitution.

One afternoon I came home to be greeted by a household in turmoil. Josh, who on the whole accepted the new rival for his mother's affections with his customary equanimity, had suddenly taken umbrage at the notion of Mo feeding his brother from what he clearly still considered to be *his* bottle. Striding over the floor of the living room he dashed it out of his brother's gums with one of his giant hands. Onto the floor it crashed. Tim broke into a wail; Josh was jumping up and down and screaming and Mo herself was in floods of tears as civilisation fell in tatters around her. Winkle the cat, who after all had more reason than any to feel displaced, was charging round demented. I stood on the threshold transfixed.

They were different in temperament, the lads. Once into solids Josh was happy to be fed and made very little mess. He was more concerned with outcome than delivery. Almost from the word go Tim, by contrast was chiefly concerned about independence: he would struggle for control of the spoon and administer its contents in roughly equal proportions to mouth, face and the rest of Yorkshire. Josh uttered not a word until he was about two-and-a-half, and soon after was delivering sentences. Tim on the other hand made himself understood from an early age but couldn't handle complete sentences until his second year at university – though boy, didn't he make up for the slow start! Tim was always self-reliant but Josh needed a friend; he found one in a mysterious being called 'Zoomzy'. Zoomzy as we discovered later, turned out to be the metal clasp that held open the sitting room window next door!

In these pre-school years we would take bits of afternoons off to go to the coast or up to the Moors. Both boys grew up with a love for the countryside. Josh also developed a passion for things mechanical. His first love was locks and he would wander round the house with an old lock and key in his hand chanting 'lock-a-lock, lock-a-lock, and lock-a-lock'. Once, when we visited Nathan and his new young wife in Leeds, Josh managed to lock their kitchen door and lose the key so that come tea time Nathan had to go out into the garden and climb in through the window to get the door open. This fascination with knowing how things worked would prove a blessing later. At the age of eleven Josh installed an entire electric circuit in the garage, with me acting as his labourer.

The boys saw a good deal of their grandparents. In those early summers we would go down to Lincolnshire, stay for a week and offload the boys onto Henry and Doreen to take in a few concerts at the King's Lynn Music Festival. Christmas and New Year were shared between Fulton and the Isle of Dogs. Weekend trips to London were rarer but my parents would come to see us from time to time. Mo always regarded these visits with trepidation, since my mum's house-keeping standards were somewhat more rigorous than ours. The next-door neighbour, keeper of Zoomzy, seeing me beating the carpets one morning, asked Mo if she was expecting her mother-in-law. How did she guess? Well, she said, we obviously considered my mum's visits as a kind of mixture of visitations by the Queen Mother and the Spanish Inquisition.

My mind had been focussed mainly on domestic events during these years but not entirely to the exclusion of university matters. The Politics Department, bereft of Ralph Alders who was still in the USA, had at last moved from its little house to the new Social Science building – altogether more spacious and salubrious – known by all as The Kremlin. What's more, Raif had asked me to teach his third-year course *Theory and Practice of British Politics* in his absence. Though this represented recognition of my general competence to teach I still hadn't found a niche for myself, an area of the discipline of Politics that I could call my own, that I would be happy researching and teaching for the rest of my career, assuming some opportunity in politics or public administration didn't jump out at me. Most academics built their specialism on the back of their PhD research, but an expertise in New Zealand education politics wasn't of much use in Britain.

One lunchtime I found myself in a lengthy discussion with Paul Johnson about the political views of George Orwell, an author whose main works I had devoured in New Zealand. Now Paul was the organiser of the Politics Society, popular with staff and students, which met regularly in a local pub and invited speakers to give an address. He invited me to address the Society on Orwell. I couldn't dodge this, but as soon as I began to put my thoughts together I felt increasingly trepidatious. It became clear that I was working in *terra incognita*. Nobody in a British Politics Department was researching or teaching in this area. After all, imaginative literature was clearly neither political 'science' nor political philosophy. How does the literature bit interact with the politics bit? That, I suddenly thought, is how I would start my paper. I would explore the relation between politics and imaginative literature using Orwell as an example. Things began to fall into place.

The talk was scheduled for a Tuesday night in February, a night that turned out to be full of snow. Nevertheless the room was heaving with students and staff when I arrived; nearly everyone I wanted to be there was there. But also there, immediately in front of me as I came in, standing against the bar with some friends, was a distinctly disdainful looking workman in brown overalls. He stood about six feet two, had spiky black hair, a thin face and baleful brown eyes, and he sported a pencil moustache. Jesus, Mary and Joseph – it was Orwell! My heart stopped. I had to rush to the toilet and get myself a drink of water. I calmed down, convincing myself that after more than twenty years George would hardly be likely to have risen up from the dead, travelled two hundred miles up to Yorkshire on a snowy night just to sneer at me. Well, no, but on the other hand, if it wasn't Orwell, who the Hell was it? Never mind, deep breath: onwards and upwards! The evening turned out to be a success, or so it seemed to me, but when it came to questions, who should ask the first but Orwell's ghost? How would I respond to the criticism, he asked, that whatever Orwell had to say about 'decency' in political life had been said more eloquently over fifty years earlier by Tolstoy? Now that's what in soccer you'd call a two-footed tackle. I staggered into a survey of my limited knowledge of Tolstoy, wrapping it round with references to Orwell. No other question was so robust and by the end I kind of knew it had gone well and that I'd managed to establish myself with my colleagues as having something to say. What had begun as an exercise in damage limitation turned out to be a *major* personal breakthrough and I owed it to Paul.

Ralph Alders had heard about the evening and asked to see a copy of the paper on Orwell. He returned it with some observations and recommended a suitable journal for publication. Some months later it was accepted without alteration. In the meantime Paul asked me if I had interests in any other writer, and promptly signed me up to give a second paper, this time on Bernard Shaw. Over the winter of 1970 I read widely to extend my somewhat spasmodic knowledge of the man. His productivity was almost as enormous as his ego and his intellectual interests were vast. About 120 years before Yuval Harari got round to the idea Shaw suggested that man would soon control his own evolution. When I came to give my paper the venue had to be changed so that more could attend: Shaw's popularity, not mine. No ghosts this time!

By early 1973 we began to think that it was time to be considering a move back to The Avenues, and a bigger house. One rainy Sunday we looked at a solidly-built, semi-detached, five-bedroom house in red brick that resembled a down-at-heel guest house. Mo wasn't drawn to it, but I persuaded her of its potential. So we put an offer in and it was accepted. We got £8,500 for our own house and our new house was £12,000. Just before the start of the new university term in 1973 we left our East Riding home. 'Bye, bye Old House,' said the boys looking back out of the rear windows as we drove off towards Hull, in the wake of the removal van, and they waved as if to a friend.

Mo and I were taking away happy memories too. It's true that life generally had been difficult. Following a confrontation with the miners the Heath government had declared a three-day working week and cut power: we were without electricity for part of the day for a good while. Then we were threatened with petrol rationing as oil prices escalated. But in the East Riding times had been kind. The house had been good to us and we had responded: we'd decorated it throughout, wallpapering ceilings for the first and last time; enlarged the kitchen by knocking down a wall and removing a toilet (I had acted as labourer to a local small builder); installed a picture window overlooking the garden and put in *real* oil-fired central heating. Moreover it was here that I had discovered a passion for writing about politics and literature, which gave me great satisfaction and earned me some kudos with my colleagues. And much more important than any of this, we had become a family. We joined in: 'bye, bye Old House – and thank you!'

Ch.10: *Home and Hearth*

Never for a moment did I think we would own such a grand house – well, a house with such potential. All the same it was semi-detached and adjoined a small Catholic children's home. Naturally we had researched this institution before buying and the general consensus was favourable: the nun in charge ran a tight ship and we wouldn't find our neighbours a problem. Neither we did – for several years.

The plan was to get the place more or less shipshape over that first weekend and so, in the teeth of Robert Nagy's charge of treason, I forsook Hull City's game at Boothferry Park on the Saturday. He was adamant: 'Look, your house'll still be there tomorrow, and the day after tomorrow. This game's a one-off; you can wait a thousand years, it'll never happen again! Where's your sense of proportion?' I stood firm. However, just before kick-off, when I was carrying stuff over to the garage for storing, a voice spoke to me, as if from just over my shoulder: 'Good afternoon ladies and gentlemen. Welcome to Boothferry Park.' Nagy had invoked The Other Side! Actually it turned out to be a bizarre trick of the wind and never happened again, but at the time it was uncanny.

In truth, I *had* been tempted to join Nagy, having forged an unexpectedly strong connection with City a few months earlier. I'd started to play league squash for the University and in summer, the off-season, I would keep fit by running round the sports fields in my heavy walking boots. Some days the City players would come to the university grounds to train, for a change of scenery. When this happened there would be a sign on the door of the main changing room. On this particular morning, when I came in from my three-mile run, there was no sign on the door, so in I strode. The room was full of naked footballers one of whom was bent over, drying a foot on a bench by the door. I caught him side on. The figure span half round, facing me as it spiralled downward. To my utter amazement I was looking into the face of none other than Thomas Henderson Docherty, ex-manager of Chelsea... and Rotherham... and Queen's Park Rangers... and Aston Villa... and FC Porto. What on earth was The Doc doing here? It transpired that he had joined City that very day, as assistant manager to Hull's young player-manager Terry Neill. The freshly installed assistant manager sprang up at me, fists raised. My profuse apologies placated my would-be assassin and he soon calmed down. We bumped into each other on a number of occasions after that, more figuratively, and talked squash and football. Docherty didn't stay long. He told me later, when we met by chance, that he had a fall-out with Terry Neil. No surprise there: The Doc hadn't come into this world to play second fiddle. That incident, though, turned me into a City fan.

That first weekend in the new house would be the first of many weekends when Hull's teams would have to do without me. For the next year I would do only what I had to do in the Department, would restrict my research and reading to what was necessary, cut most of my sporting attendances, and give over all my spare time to modernising and redecorating the house. That weekend was spent shifting furniture in advance of my first big job: the removal of a downstairs fireplace. With the furniture in place I set to work with a sledgehammer.

After the fireplace I concentrated on upstairs. The first job was to take out another fireplace, in the bedroom at the back of the house, shovelling the rubble straight out of the back window. Both of the boys were intrigued by the work and Josh wanted to help. Could he shift the rubble round to the side of the house where a pile of the waste was burgeoning? Why not? After all, he had a trolley that normally held his wooden bricks and a plastic spade. Josh shovelled one brick at a time on to his trolley and when he had four he would trundle them round to the growing pile at the side of the house and come back for more. He did this for the whole of one Saturday before going to bed and sleeping for a month. The bedroom walls were painted, the toilets and bathroom were pine-clad and painted, and finally the upstairs hall and the stairwell were papered and that involved a drop of fifteen feet, which Mo and I managed together on planks loaned to us by a decorator friend. My *pièce de résistance* was Josh's bedroom. I built a unit in pine incorporating a bed, a wardrobe and cupboard with drawers. One day when Josh was at play school I painted a cascade of flowers on the wall above and around the bedhead: red poppies, white roses, bluebells, and lots of jungular vegetation. It was a triumph. When Josh came home he went up to his room directly. We heard a strangulated yell: 'Scrape it off! Scrape it off!'

Next two large downstairs rooms, a sitting and a dining room were painted and the carpets replaced. Now for the big stuff. Prior to getting central heating installed we decided that the back of the house needed major work. Cousin David, who had shown so little drawing ability as a child – so I thought – had gone on to gain a First Class Honours degree in Architecture and was now a practicing architect in Liverpool. He came over to tell us which walls I could safely knock down. I decided to launch the enterprise on the Saturday of June 1st, sometime around 3.30pm when everyone would be out for a couple of hours, by removing a wall. I started with more misgivings than students could have squeezed into a Mini. After about an hour, when I'd made a man-sized hole in the wall, I heard a dreadful rumble. I was transfixed, riveted to the spot, my heart pumping like a steam hammer, waiting for the entire ceiling to fall in on me. Then, just as suddenly, nothing: no disaster. At a chemical plant at Flixborough, south of the Humber, where they manufactured cyclohexane for nylon, there had been a massive explosion – the equivalent of fifteen tonnes of TNT. Eighteen lives were lost that afternoon. That explosion had coincided precisely with my hammer blow.

Now ceilings had to be restored and floors levelled, and for a month or two that part of the house was like a building site. Anything but easy for Mo, looking after two young children in those circumstances, especially since two of my colleagues came to help and had to be fed and watered. But we managed – and what a difference! It took about three years to finish all the work we wanted to do on the house but that first year saw it transformed from a large, solidly built, cold, dampish, inconvenient and dismally decorated small guest house into a bright family home with central heating. Time to be getting back to my proper job.

There had been big changes in the Politics Department that year. Ralph Alders had finally decided to quit his social work in the north and to head for the leafy south-west. In his place came Wilfred Potts from Anglesey, a short, burly man with a bulbous nose, wiry grey hair and a glass eye who had previously been a senior lecturer at Cardiff. To his colleagues Potts looked a bit like a garden gnome but what Potts himself saw in the mirror was Napoleon. His task was to rid the Department of sloth and rebellion and he acted decisively from the beginning. Coming

114

back from a late Senate meeting one Wednesday, the story went, he'd opened the departmental office door to find his pert, willowy secretary on the floor with her knickers off, her exquisite breasts exposed and her fine young legs wrapped around a colleague's neck. Potts curtly informed both that neither had a future at Hull. Napoleon was going to expand the Department considerably over the next few years: Hull was going places, he said, and he was as good as his word.

For me these years were professionally disastrous. My PhD thesis had been accepted for publication in New Zealand in a revised format and I'd worked on it on and off for two years, along with the house restoration. Suddenly the publisher got cold feet. I was informed by my old squash-playing mate, a senior educationalist that new strategic alliances had been formed and that information I had accumulated, were it now to come into the public domain, would cause considerable embarrassment and maybe worse. Be satisfied with publishing a few articles from your revised thesis was my friend's advice. Reluctantly I followed it. Years later I discovered that my thesis had become widely consulted in New Zealand, though by consenting adults in private. All the same, my thesis did have its uses from the beginning: it proved exactly the right height for balancing my mum's washing horse in front of the fire.

Worse followed. Wilfred Potts persuaded me to organise a series of seminars on the Politics of Education. It would be good, he said, to bring a series of 'big names' to the Department and I would be able to publish a collection of papers with myself as editor. Potts assured me that with prestigious contributors, he, Potts, would be able to secure publication through his professional contacts. I went ahead reluctantly. Contributors including a number of leading authorities in the field and a politician were recruited. The latter attracted a large audience one Friday afternoon but failed to turn up. Telephone calls to his office revealed he had left with his secretary at lunchtime: he was to spend the weekend at the Hull Politics Department. *Really?* One senior politician, one car, one secretary and one free weekend – and no seminar paper: what could possibly have happened?

Collecting and editing these contributions was time-consuming but finally I presented the completed manuscript to Potts. Well, he said, why not appoint an agent to seek out the best deal? If this failed – and it wouldn't – Potts would step in. After the agent had elicited refusals from five or six publishers, he returned the manuscript, along with the reviews which ranged from the positive to the enthusiastic, but each concluded that this was not the time to be publishing edited collections in relatively uncharted territory. I took the agent's letter to Potts only to discover that he had no friends in publishing after all. He had had in mind the editor of Hull's own University Press, Philip Larkin, no friend of Potts, nor of anybody much. Larkin had established a reputation for enjoying a colourful social life – one of my colleagues was a neighbour and could vouch for this – but a dour professional one. I hardly knew the man myself. The summer before we had had a run-in when I had been charged for an overdue library book. My explanation, that I had been overseas on university business and so unable to return the book was dismissed by Britain's finest living poet with complete disdain. In my experience in his professional life he was a bureaucrat in every sense and I was not optimistic.

I was to draft a letter to Larkin explaining our predicament but first to show it Potts. My draft was hapless, said Potts, *far* too self-deprecating and negative: I should tell Larkin what an outstanding collection we had and how its publication would enhance Hull UP's reputation. Reluctantly I recast the letter and whilst not beating any drums, made it more positive, quoting the reviews. Potts thought this was *just about* positive enough and off the letter went. The following week I heard back: Hull University Press, wrote Larkin smugly (well, I'm guessing), operated chiefly to support in-house work that, though academically worthy, was not a good commercial bet. From what I'd written, our proposal clearly needed no such support. End of story. I have no doubt Potts thought he had been acting for the best, for me and for the Department, and with better luck things might have turned out well. But he had been economical with the truth all along.

The two major enterprises that I'd struggled to find time for in my busy building and decorating schedule had failed. The only plus from this period was a third seminar paper to the Politics Society, this time on HG Wells, and again the paper was well attended and seemed to be well received, and again I subsequently had no problem in getting it published. On the back of this Paul Johnson suggested I consider putting on an Honours course on politics and literature. Now why hadn't I thought of that? My course could be called *Socialism and Literature* and could include writers who addressed themes that directly or indirectly bore upon the rise and decline of socialism in Britain. I would start with the utopian William Morris, then the Fabian Bernard Shaw, the scientist HG Wells, then after the First War, when scepticism set in, Aldous Huxley, Arthur Koestler and George Orwell, finishing with that pessimistic take on the human condition *Lord of the Flies*. I took my (rather Paul's) idea to Potts; he bought it. It took over a year to prepare the course thoroughly but finally it appeared as an Honours Option and I had no trouble recruiting students. Although in coming unstuck with politics and education I could hardly be said to have lost an empire, in politics and literature I had definitely found a role. For the rest of my career I felt like a professional footballer being paid to do what I loved; only maybe not so much.

What's more, I later began work on a book which would prove handy for students taking my course, as well, naturally, as being absolutely groundbreaking. Eventually I submitted my plan to a major publisher and it was accepted. For three months or so before it came out I would waken in a muck-sweat from the same dream: someone was about to publish a book with a similar theme before me! But that didn't happen, and one day in the spring of 1979 my author's copy came through the post. How could the world ever be the same again?

But somehow it managed: nobody noticed! I discussed this with my greengrocer who, with a keener strategic sense, suggested murdering Mo and cutting her into pieces. When arrested I could offhandedly let it be known that I'd written a book. Sure to sell like hot cakes. It wasn't a bad book: my mum showed it around. I sent a copy to my old History teacher Kenneth Rennie and received a moving reply from his wife. Kenneth was almost blind now but she had read the book to him and he had enjoyed it very much. Something had definitely changed: I began to accept that my future lay in the university world and not in the world of politics or administration.

We didn't spend all these years working. By now we had an allotment – this was the age of *The Good Life,* self-sufficiency, that sort of thing. I spent hours in communion with vegetables.

Holidays played a big part in our family life and continued to do so until the boys left home: we camped. The boys shared their parents' interests: they thrilled to see castles, they enjoyed long walks and they liked quiet beaches. When Mo and I decided on a walk the boys invariably wanted to visit a castle; when a visit to a castle was on the agenda they would argue for a day by the sea…and so on. Nevertheless we were able to do things that filled in spaces left empty in my own childhood. Later we took our main holiday with another family in a series of large gîtes around rural France. We wanted to give our children the kind of holidays they would always look back on with fondness and I think we did. I have no such happy memories of my own childhood.

Meanwhile in the big outside world, times they were a-changing. The 1960s had carried us, like everyone else, into new cultural territory. We were sympathetic to the decriminalisation of homosexuality, the abolition of the death penalty, even reform of the abortion laws. The proletarianisation of popular culture that had begun in the previous decade was reinforced by the success of the Beatles and the Stones. Fine! But the revolution didn't stop there. By the 1970s Punk Rock arrived, and soon after came the Skinheads, white power and the Oi! Bands. Beards and long hair, flowery shirts and flared trousers were giving way to shaved skulls, belts and braces and Doc Marten boots; second-wave feminism was aggressively challenging traditional assumptions about women and society and nudity was rife in the theatre. Where was it all going?

And we now had problems of our own. A substantial rise in mortgage rates left us pretty well broke. There was nothing for it: Mo would have to go back to teaching. So back she went resignedly to teach French in a Junior High School out in East Hull, and though she found it hard she made some lifelong friends there and came quite to enjoy it. It became my job to take the boys to and from school and to feed them at lunchtimes – and those lads were growing up. Thought would soon have to be given to their secondary education. A table of national educational performance that didn't have Hull at the bottom had yet to be invented and our best bet, if our boys were to have as good an education as ours, seemed to be a local private day school. Josh took the entry test and passed with flying colours. We did our calculations; assuming Tim would pass the following year, which he did; we would just about be able to manage with Mo's salary.

Perhaps this wasn't the best time to think about extending the family but for a while I had been suggesting to Mo that we should try for a third child. She set two conditions: she wanted a girl and a new washing machine. I promised both. In the autumn Mo duly became pregnant again. She would need a bedroom, our new daughter, so we tried to persuade Tim, in the small bedroom next to ours, to move to the large guest bedroom at the back of the house. No, not unless I painted a Viking on the wall. Well, I promised...

That winter of 1978-79, the Winter of Discontent, saw the Labour government's statutory incomes policy collapse followed by widespread strikes. Empty supermarket shelves, piles of rubbish in the streets, bodies going unburied. An election was due the following May and to my disbelief and dismay Margaret Thatcher won. I took to the back bedroom for the following week and painted not just one Viking but a whole boatload of Vikings marauding across the bedroom wall, setting a village ablaze. Thatcher inspired me.

120

Then, on June 8th 1979, I was present at the birth of Kathleen Louise Spring. Seeing our boys for the very first time had been magical but this was the greatest experience of my life. Not only was I *there* but I deployed my weight-training experience to help Mo with her breathing. In fact the midwife was so impressed she asked me if I was for hire. From the moment Kathleen Louise poked her nose into the world and decided it was safe to come out she brought joy with her, and there aren't many people you can say that about. Such delicate, expertly chiselled fingers, such smiley eyes, such a sweet face. Kathleen's brothers weren't quite so enthusiastic: 'Oh no; not a *girl!*'

Ch.11: *Dark Clouds, Silver Linings*

Every silver lining has a dark cloud. Sister Frances, in charge of the children's home next door, was moving on. The Diocesan authority at Middlesbrough had decided that financial support from the local authority was required and this, in turn, would mean accepting some local authority children. Would our neighbours continue to be as quiet, polite and friendly? For some time the changes seemed to work out rather well. The former second-in-command, Isabel, a young woman in her thirties ruled with just as firm a hand. Some of her new charges were boisterous and, being non-Catholics, less constrained by threats of eternal damnation. Terry, for example, knocked Josh off his bike one afternoon and rode off on it. 'Why did he do that?' Josh complained. 'If he'd wanted a go on my bike, he should've asked: I'd have let him!' Josh hadn't heard of the 'clash of civilisations' theory. In the early summer of 1979, however, Isabel had caused uproar by accusing a local man of having a relationship with one of her charges. Was this the cause of what happened subsequently? That summer, a few weeks after Kathleen arrived, our domestic tranquillity blew up.

The boys from next door were away in Wales and Isabel had been staying on her own. Now young Kathleen Spring, occupying the room next to ours, had slept right through the night from the first. That's probably why her coughing had immediately wakened her mum in the early hours of an August Sunday. Mo woke me: was that smoke she could smell? I leapt from the bed, told Mo to collect the baby and immediately woke the boys. In a matter of minutes we were all out in the front garden and the fire

123

brigade was on its way. At this point, with the family safe, I went back and one after another carefully opened the downstairs doors. Must be next door, I told the firemen. The downstairs rooms next door had been doused in paraffin and a burning rag had been tossed in. For some unaccountable reason the paraffin had smouldered but not ignited: hence the smoke and fumes which had penetrated the walls. In all probability, said the firemen, Kathleen's discreet coughing had saved us. Isabel had been the target but thank God she hadn't spent the night there. Though there had been little structural damage in the home it needed extensive redecoration and the children wouldn't be coming back for some months.

Not a pleasant feeling to know that someone has attempted to kill your neighbour and that you might have departed this world as collateral damage. For me what really mattered was the family. It was necessary for the boys' sake to play the incident down, not to react in such a way as to frighten them. I found it easy enough to get the boys' minds off the events, but it was more difficult for Mo. She was fraught with anxiety. Things got slowly better over the next few weeks but her tension surrounded her like an aura. Fortunately we had a holiday planned in the North York Moors. Kathleen was absolutely no problem and the boys had a beck to play in and ducks and chickens to victimise. *The Blacksmith's Arms* was very welcoming after a walk and there was a grocery store which doubled as a post office where the boys could be sent to get a paper in the mornings with money for sweets. We were due to leave on the Saturday and on the Friday evening Mo cooked the boys' favourite meal, roast chicken. I left the wishbone on a mantel shelf to dry as ever, just as my parents had. Mo and I would pull it later and the one who got the bigger part got a wish.

124

We'd packed the car on the Saturday morning and were just tidying when I remembered the wishbone. We pulled it and the lucky bit shot out across the floor leaving us both with tiny slivers. Mo joked she hoped that wasn't an omen.

Back in Hull again we seemed to have turned a corner. There was no acrid smell in the house and there were plenty of things to be done to prepare for the new term. Next morning Mo and I had gone over the road with Kathleen to have coffee with friends when Josh appeared to tell us that Mr. Gregory was on the phone. Now Mr. Gregory was the Oliver's next door neighbour; something must have happened to Henry. The news was as bad as it could be: Henry had died that morning of a heart attack. Another bolt from the blue. Poor Mo; she had hardly got over the fire. We had to drive down, the boys staying with friends for the day. I left Mo, who was still breast-feeding Kathleen, in Fulton with her mother, doing what had to be done; Doreen would be in pieces. I had gained a great affection for Henry, though in just about every respect we were different. Over the previous twelve years, since our return from New Zealand, Henry and I had often been out for a drink at the local Constitutional Club and I came to feel very much at ease in his company, with the reassuring smell of his snuff – Wilson's of Sheffield – scenting the air as we sat chewing the fat: we got on. As for Mo, she had always been far closer to her father than her mother; they were more alike. She was devastated.

Henry would be badly missed by his grandsons. Josh and Tim would love to go down to his workshop where he operated two lathes. Henry made Josh a dynamo once which, when wound up quickly, would light up a small electric bulb. He had fixed it rather shambolically to a rough oil-stained wooden block. I took it off, sanded the block, inscribed it, varnished it and polished the dynamo before putting it back together. Josh has it still. Had Henry lived another five years or more both boys would have got so much from him in the way of understanding how things work. He was seventy-seven when he died, no age for Lincolnshire. I never pulled another wishbone.

The funeral was held on a warm autumn day and Henry was buried within a stone's throw of his workshop – if our Tim had done the throwing anyway – in the graveyard behind St. Mark's where Mo and I had been married fifteen years earlier. Henry had done odd jobs for so many of the local farmers and businessmen over the years and many of them came to see him off. One laid a wreath made in the shape of a micrometer. Mo and I arranged for the sale of his car and his equipment and before long his workshop was an empty shell. Indeed that's just how Henry himself had been when I saw him laid out: the real Henry was away. We had a small reception back at the house. James had been good enough to drive up from Essex to represent the family. Doreen handled herself remarkably well, a portent of an unanticipated ability to reshape her life and make the most of things. Just as well because she was to survive Henry by a quarter of a century.

Soon the boys and Mo were back into the routine of school and the fear of the fire and the grief at Henry's death slowly melted away. We had been visited by a priest from Middlesbrough who wanted to explain to us why they intended to re-establish the home. I told him that our personal preference would have been for the house to be sold but we appreciated the Church's position and supported its stance on principle. Nevertheless, I pointed out, it was we Springs who were in the front line, and we really needed a guarantee that there should always, *always*, be an adult on duty in the house. Father Smith gave an absolute undertaking that this would be so.

Meanwhile work was being undertaken in restoring the property and a couple of weeks before Christmas an article appeared in the local paper concluding that all was ready and the children would be back in before Christmas. Mo was delighted; having a large empty house next door left her permanently on edge. Four days before Christmas I woke before 7am to strange noises. What struck me immediately was how light it seemed to be for mid-winter and almost immediately I realised that this was because fire was spurting out of an upstairs window next door and the noises I'd heard were crashing timber. Another quick but disciplined exodus and the fire brigade arrived if anything even quicker than last time. This time the arsonist had done a much better job and though the firemen soon had the blaze under control much of the interior of the house was already gutted. The fire had spread into our loft and roofers had to come and make our roof good with tarpaulin. The shattered downstairs windows of the home were boarded up.

There was much to be organised and rearranged that awful morning and it was several hours before I could sit down. I found myself in the front room alone and in despair, wondering how on earth Mo could manage this new body blow. Quite suddenly I became acutely aware of an unmistakable smell: it was Henry's snuff. I don't doubt there are many rational explanations for this but I was and remain happy to consider it part of what Richard Holloway called the 'mystery of being'.

That was a long, hard Christmas and though the Church authorities were quick to say that they would now sell the house as soon as it had been restored, Mo was inconsolable. How often over the next couple of years would I waken in the morning to feel a body as rigid as a board next to me, see eyes staring fixedly at the ceiling, nerves screwed up to near breaking point. Mo was desperate to move but as I explained, to sell the house, if it were possible, which I doubted, would be to make an unrecoverable loss. Bringing up a young family and preparing her new term's teaching helped Mo, but it was touch and go over the next few months. Nevertheless, however hard these years were for her, between us we managed to ensure that our anxieties didn't affect the boys. Watching them grow and take on the world, basking in the joy that their little sister brought to the household was what sustained us. Things slowly got better: windows replaced the boards next door and finally the house was put on the market. The nightmare was all but over. In due course, in the spring of 1983, a couple, who owned a restaurant in town, moved in with the parents of one. It was such a relief to have the house occupied and a positive delight to see the garden tamed.

It was about this time that I decided to have my shoulder fixed. I had played my final game of rugby sixteen years earlier in New Zealand. It was the last match of the season and I had gone into a heavy tackle and come out in considerable pain in the right shoulder. At just that point the ball went into touch and the game ended. For the next few months I cradled my right elbow in my left hand whenever possible. Slowly the discomfort went. Much later, after an X-ray in Hull, my doctor told me that my collar collarbone had been shattered and needed fixing. Let's get you on the waiting list, he said. But he forgot. A few years later we joined a private health scheme through a special offer at the University;

it made sense to put it to use, especially since there was a small private hospital not 100 yards from our house. So in the spring of 1983 I went in and had the various pieces of collarbone collected together. A piece of bone was taken from my hip and a metal plate was inserted to brace this reconstruction. It was surprisingly painful, especially the hip, and stayed so for a month or more. I had secretly hoped a stronger shoulder would transform my squash, but sad to say it made not the slightest difference.

While I was in hospital recovering from the operation one of my squash colleagues paid me a visit. Roger Ablett was a warden of one of the University's halls of residence out in the East Riding. There were six more or less identical halls on a site known as The Briars. One of the wardens was about to retire and the senior warden had asked Roger to sound me out; he thought that I could 'do a job'. Though I said I would think about it, it didn't seem to be my kind of thing. However, when I mentioned it to Mo she jumped at the idea. So we went to visit the retiring warden in his house on The Briars. It was an architect-designed house and very appealing, but all the same I didn't fancy the job. Mo was surprisingly positive but then I twigged: it would mean a move away from her nightmare! With considerable misgivings I applied for the wardenship and was successful. We would move in the late summer of 1983. The prospect of having to run a hall of residence with 140 testosterone-filled lads did not appeal to me one bit but I owed it to Mo.

So: a house to be sold, with considerable attraction for anyone who wanted a floor-to-ceiling picture of a Viking raid. Good friends had asked could they have first refusal on the house: they bought it for £48,000. Now, the house at The Briars was rent free, which meant that we had to consider what to do with the profits from the sale of our own house. We decided that after repaying our mortgage we would look for a cottage in the North York Moors or the Dales.

One Wednesday in autumn I took Tim and Kathleen, both recovering from colds, up to Swaledale to look at cottages. We looked at three, the best of which was one of a renovated terrace of three with an intriguing history. The address was The Norse Longhouse, and that's exactly what it had been. It was, we discovered, the last heather-thatched cottage in the Dales. We later got hold of a picture from *The Dalesman* taken in the early twentieth century showing a sturdy whitewashed cottage with a sturdy soap-washed housewife at the door. In the 1970s a local builder had acquired a few such old properties, pulled them down, put in a damp course and solid fuel central heating, rebuilt them in the modern style, with the original material where possible, and re-roofed them with Hardraw slabs. They were about as weather-proof as could be, an important consideration up on the edge of the world.

The children took to it straight away, possibly swayed by the chocolate cake and ice cream the owner offered them, and though I would have preferred the original for architectural and historical reasons, I recognised this modern incarnation was eminently sensible; Mo would have to come to see it. On Remembrance Sunday we made the trip, stopping for coffee in Richmond where, in brilliant autumn sunshine we saw the Green Howards on parade. Like the rest of the family Mo came, saw and was conquered. We decided there and then to take the plunge and by the end of 1983 the longhouse was ours. One very snowy Saturday in January we hired a van and took up some hastily acquired furniture, which had to be carried about 20 yards from the road because the snow was too deep. Almost immediately two neighbours appeared to help and stayed on for a cup of tea. One turned out to be a Chemisty lecturer from Durham University, the other a tenant farmer, a Hungarian, whose house stood on the next ridge about a quarter of a mile away. By dinner time the family was settled and the house almost warm. Our first night in that silent white world was wonderfully cosy.

Next morning our new Hungarian friend reappeared. Imre had come out in 1956, just like Robert Nagy and again like Robert he spoke no English. Fate had taken him to Sunderland where he learnt his 'English': on first acquaintance he was practically incomprehensible. For all that he was one of the nicest men I've met and one of the smartest. If we planned to come up on Friday evening for the weekend, Imre would go down and light a fire a couple of hours before we arrived. His house abutted a hillside and was perpetually damp so for his birthday one year he bought a second-hand JCB for £150 and removed the hillside. He could do almost anything that involved machines or motors and had a wide knowledge of country lore and taught Tim how to snare rabbits. On his first attempt Tim caught two. Imre died about five years later from a brain haemorrhage and without him that part of the world lost a little bit of its magic.

The Norse Longhouse was a remote spot. The Romans had mined lead up there, as had others, up to late Victorian times. Lead spoils and small furnace chimneys dotted the landscape. The fields and the fells were broken up by isolated and often deserted farms with tumbled-down outbuildings. Armies of gritty black-faced Swaledales kept watch over this gnarled landscape. Intermittently the call of curlews, or the chatter of red grouse, normally invisible unless you happened to tread on one, pierced the air. In August their chatter became distraught cries as they strove against the guns. We found it necessary to sell the cottage in 1992, after more than eight years. What a wrench! We'd become part of the place, going to Mass in the local village hall; attending local functions; patronising *The Black Bull*; walking the moors around Reeth, Gunnerside and Muker; frequenting the local markets on market days. We voted in the Richmond by-election in 1988 when a certain William Hague was elected. We loved it. Yet had it not been for that ghastly fire we would never have experienced the joy of living, if only intermittently, in the wild, gaunt hills above the Swale and the Arkle. Truly this is God's own County. As they say, every dark cloud has its silver lining.

Ch.12: *In Charge of the Asylum*

'No university could afford this today,' said cousin David the architect: 'every brick on this site has been hand cast.' Six almost identical halls, designed by Gillespie, Kidd and Coia in 1967, had won awards, and were set in an area of parkland dotted with specimen trees: it was a delightful place to live. All the same, it wouldn't have mattered if the bricks had been gold: I was not enamoured of The Briars. For me its most significant feature was the 135 testosterone-filled young men whom I had no desire whatever to oversee. Each of the six halls was managed by a warden, one of whom, the senior warden, had overall responsibility for the site. It was he, Brian Harper, who had thought of me as a potential warden. When advising me how I should go about the job he revealed that, being deaf in one ear he always slept on his good ear – what my dad would have called 'cocking a deaf 'un'. That way, problems always either solved themselves or came in the mornings. I couldn't be so sanguine; for the first month I would stay up each night till past 1am just in case something happened. And if I heard a noise I would go and investigate.

Sometimes a great deal of noise was on the agenda. Each hall had five blocks and each block held an 'official' party every year. Built on three levels, each with a small communal space the set-up was not conducive to partying unless enough noise was generated to engulf much of the western world. I approached the first such 'block party' in my hall with some misgivings. I had installed a Cambridge graduate who had just started on a PhD in Chemistry as my deputy; a pleasant man but not one to bang heads. On the night in question I had asked him to go over when the party was in full swing to minimise criminality. Just after 12.30pm two students knocked on my door: would I come and extricate my deputy? Some lads from another hall had him stuck in the main door and were slowly crushing him to death. I did so and took the opportunity to remind the students that parties ended at 1am, i.e. ten minutes or so later. I was certain of this rule since I'd made it up on the way over. Aside from these official ones no party was allowed without the warden's permission and mine was sought only once; for a birthday party held in A Block at 4pm on a Sunday afternoon when only Tizer was drunk and fish paste sandwiches, blancmange, sherry trifle and strawberry jelly were consumed. Just to add a touch of authenticity one of the female guests was sick. Could it possibly have been Violet Elizabeth Bott?

The main threat to civil order however came from large events organised for the whole site. Entertainment and food were mostly provided at The Briars Centre with facilities for approximately a thousand students. Periodically groups or bands would be hired and some attracted large audiences who would naturally consume considerable quantities of alcohol. Worst of all were the 'Oompah' bands: by 8.30pm in the evenings they would have their largely male audiences dancing on the tables with their trouser legs rolled up. When the Centre closed a stream of legless storm troopers would pour out onto the site wondering how they could extend the evening's entertainment. Now each warden was required to take responsibility for the whole site, all six halls, for one evening each week, so that others warden could go out. In that first year I was in charge on Tuesdays and as luck would have it, one Tuesday night was Oompah Night, so it fell to me to try to break up the heaving mass that emerged from the Centre at chucking-out time and channel it to the relevant halls. When I stood in front of this tumultuous rag bag army and told some of them to peel off and go to their own hall, they stood swaying, glowering, muttering, like some great slavering beast, and I realised that they were debating whether to do as requested or sweep me contemptuously aside and continue to the next hall *en masse*. It was touch and go but finally they peeled off. I was so wound up that though I'd managed the situation I didn't sleep afterwards: only after a few years in the job would I be able to handle these situations confidently. That first year as a warden was tough but it did finally come to an end. In fact students were in residence for only thirty weeks of the year so there were long periods when The Briars was a very congenial place to be. And more so when three of the wardens were replaced by people I happened to know and get on with.

I had to get on top of this job. My responsibility, as I saw it, was to ensure that my hall was a place where students could work if they chose. Having a good time was their responsibility; maintaining a reasonable sense of good order was mine. One problem was that they couldn't all fit into our Hall Common Room so it was impossible to address them, and let them know what was expected of them, what the parameters of behaviour were. So from year two I started a termly newsletter. Then I created a new role: each Block would elect a spokesman and these five would meet regularly with the deputy warden and me for a beer in the deputy's flat. Student worries could be directed upwards and my concerns could be channelled down. If a student complained through his Rep about being kept awake after

10.30pm by the clatter of coffee cups – and this happened – they wouldn't get much support. On the other hand, if a Rep reported someone skateboarding down the stairs at 3am all week – and this happened too – I would act. I began the new regime by telling Block Reps that though I'd be sympathetic to requests for small events like birthdays there would be no more Block parties. I expected a revolt but there was none; in fact I think they were relieved. I was more confidently in charge now and I actually began to enjoy the job.

Four of The Briars halls were mixed, the fifth was all-female and ours all-male. There was a case for an all-female hall; the University was getting a growing number of applications from young Asian women who had, or whose parents had a strong preference for single-sex accommodation. There was no similar need for an all-male hall and in fact 90% of our inmates had applied unsuccessfully for mixed accommodation in the first instance. I was sympathetic to the notion of an eventual change of status, but two events convinced me to act sooner rather than later. Early one evening some lads from A Block informed me that as they were leaving for the pub one of their number had fallen down the stairs and might have broken his arm. Off they went to the pub. I found him on his bed sobbing, arm obviously broken, and phoned for an ambulance. The following Tuesday, my duty day, two girls from one of the mixed halls knocked on the door to report a similar event. They had sat the injured party on a chair, put a blanket round him, made him a cup of hot sweet tea and phoned for an ambulance. They just thought I'd like to know. Sparta or Athens? We needed to preference our Athenian side!

We would hold a referendum when, no doubt, a substantial majority would champion change. So in my next newsletter I

136

explained what was to happen and added that I would bring out a 'referendum special' newsletter and invited student contributions. I received a total of zero so I took it upon myself to spell out the arguments for and against. Each copy of the 'special' had a numbered tear-off voting slip at the bottom. A ballot box was positioned in the lobby outside our house. If anybody had wanted, they could have rigged the outcome but that would have taken ingenuity and energy so it wasn't going to happen. At 10pm that evening I brought in the ballot box. Of 135 students in the Hall only 65 had bothered to vote. Of these 31 (24 percent) had voted in favour of change and 34 (26 percent) had voted for the status quo. The people had spoken! I was nonplussed. I put out another newsletter headed: *We're Going Mixed – Only 26% Oppose!!* A short piece explained why this decision was good for the Hall. I would be happy to discuss the vote with anyone. Nobody came. I felt a bit like the left-wing Miners' leader who refused to hold a strike ballot. He wasn't going to be 'constitutionalised out of action'. But how did this square with my principle of democratic participation? Most of the 'the people' hadn't bothered to vote and many of those who voted wouldn't be in hall next year anyway. As for those coming in with the following intake, they couldn't be consulted, but history suggested that about 90% would prefer a mixed hall. So did 26% of a transient population present the 'wisdom of the crowd'? Anyway, I tended to agree with Beatrice Webb who couldn't understand the theory whereby multiplying ignorant opinions indefinitely you produce wisdom. We went mixed. Cycling home one late afternoon the following November with the setting sun lavishing a rich orange across the bare trees of the parkland, I heard Mozart's flute concerto in G Major floating out from C Block. On a third-floor balcony stood the flautist, the light from her room picking out her silhouette. Q.E.D.

Earlier that year one of my younger colleagues in Politics, also a warden, had interviewed a mature candidate for Honours Politics the previous spring and recommended that he be made an unconditional offer. The man in question had a history of petty crime and during his last stay in one of Her Majesty's establishments of correction, had taken an introductory Open University course and discovered a natural penchant for political thought. During his interview he had discoursed on Greek political philosophy in a strong Cockney accent. He duly took up his offer of a place and by all accounts his tutorial contributions were fascinating. My colleague had offered his protégé a place in his Hall. At a Block party at the end of the first week the gentleman in question threatened a self-appointed bouncer, a rugby man, with a flick knife. Then women in the Hall complained that he was using binoculars to spy on them in their rooms. A few weeks later he stuck his knife under the chin of the President of the Student Union. Before the term was over, by which time my colleague had decided to wash his hands of him, the lad was rusticated. Two months later this colleague received a badly-spelled, hand-written letter postmarked Dalton. It was our man and he accused his former mentor of treachery, promising to come up to Hull to cut him open. A distinctly apprehensive young warden sought my advice: should he take this letter seriously? The lad probably meant every word, I said, but would be far too busy sorting out rivals in his own parish to take the 400 mile journey up to Hull and back just to work over an academic. Unreassured the warden sought succour from Her Majesty's Constabulary to be told that they would be able to help only if the guy actually did come up and work him over. For the next six months or so my friend would open his front door only very slowly and slept in those dreaming spires of Academe with a baseball bat under the bed!

The Briars was a pleasant atmosphere for family life: the children flourished. Josh proved to be academically gifted. He passed all his O Level examinations with a string of 'A's and had entered the Sixth Form. He had wanted to mix his subjects, adding History to Biology and Chemistry, but according to the Headmaster such a mixture would bar him from entrance to a good university. I wrote to assure the Head, as a former Faculty Admissions Officer, that this was no longer true. Back came the reply: the Head didn't doubt my competence but I was after all speaking for Hull and universities like it, not for the Oxbridge colleges, or the likes of King's or UCL. So I got friends in these hallowed institutions to write telling me how they would react to an application from Josh for a science degree. Their answers were almost identical: an excellent combination as long as the grades were good. I forwarded these letters to the Head. I never did get a reply but Josh was permitted to take his mix and by the following year mixes had become almost the norm at the school.

During his first year in the VIth Josh became increasingly interested in History and at the end of the summer term he was invited down to Magdalen College Oxford for a young historians' week, along with fifteen others from around the UK. How did he react to this super opportunity? It was truly *awful*, he said; full of southern ponces; he'd never want to study there. A finely grounded judgement, we thought: the fruits of an expensive education. (Mind, he hadn't turned down the chance because Oxford wasn't in Yorkshire, like his dad.) Months later he went to Edinburgh for an Open Day and came back quite certain that *this* was the place for him and sure enough that's where he finally went to study not Sciences but History – very happily: his instincts had been right. The following autumn we drove Josh up for the start of his first term; within ten minutes of saying goodbye I had to stop the car: we were both in tears at the prospect of losing our son. I was overcome, too, by a powerful sensation: I had fulfilled my biological destiny and it was surely time to make way for the next generation This was an awful, awful day but thank goodness not to be repeated when Tim and Kathleen left later.

Tim, by comparison, was happy to cruise along at school, making a wide circle of friends, playing not too seriously for one of the school Fifteens and generally just about keeping his head above water academically. I could recognise myself, pre-VIth Form, in my younger son. Where we differed, though, was in reading: Tim didn't read much until he got older, whereas I had read a very great deal. He passed most of his GCSEs but got no high marks and drifted into the VIth. In the evenings Mo and I and the boys would work until 10pm when we would meet up and have a cup of tea and watch the *Ten O'clock News*. One evening Tim came down with a drawing he'd made of a double eagle on the back of a Goth's leather jacket. I was on the point of reminding him that he should have been working but realised immediately that our son had a talent for draftsmanship. I found a photo of the Royal Palace at Greenwich, which Tim had seen often enough in real life, and asked him to copy it. This was not Tim's cup of tea, but he made a really good fist of it. Had he ever thought of following his uncle and becoming an architect, since he was clearly more of a creative than an analytical turn of mind? Though Josh was the more academically able, as he grew up Tim was acquiring the air of a man who would succeed in the affairs of the world (where on earth had that come from?). Unfortunately he was handicapped by a belief that the gift of imagination obviated the need for hard graft. He later acquired an ability to graft with the best. On the whole these teenage years, despite some serious wobbles, passed off far better than we had the right to expect, though I had to accept that for both boys growing up included an inexorable drift away from the Church, which saddened me.

Kathleen was a bright girl, worked hard and smiled a lot. When she was four I had had to go down to London for three days to act as a character witness in the trial of a cousin, a taxi driver who had been charged with indecent assault. He was found not guilty, something that nobody who knew him would have doubted for a second, and when I got home Kathleen, lying out on the floor thumb in mouth, half-watching *Blue Peter*, asked me what I'd been doing. I explained and taking her thumb out of her mouth, Kathleen turned and said: 'That sounds cool. I think I'll be a lawyer.' When we first moved to The Briars I used to take her to playschool in Hull on the back of my bike. She asked me to pass the time by telling her all about the history of England as we went. Not easy since I had to keep turning my head round but I didn't short-change her: she got the lot, from Julius Caesar to Margaret Thatcher. Boy, was I pleased when we'd finished, until she asked me to start again. First I refused point blank, but then I softened. Still looking for a way out I agreed provided she could show she had been listening. I would ask her one question; if she answered correctly I would start again and if not I wouldn't. She agreed reluctantly. 'OK,' I said, 'so who was the last Viking king of

Yorkshire?' A fair question, since this was local history and I'd given some time to Mr. Bloodaxe and his Viking friends. Silence. Stealing a glance, I saw a lower lip protrude and start to wobble and tears begin to form. Then suddenly those eyes opened wide: 'Eric Blood Donor!' she shouted triumphantly. As she progressed through primary school it became clear that she was bright enough to be just about anything she wanted, including a lawyer, and though she got the attention of an only child, being seven years younger than Tim, she was never spoilt; her brothers saw to that.

Like so many teachers in Hull, Mo suffered at the whims of the local authority. Hull had earlier decided to create a new category of school, the middle school, and primary and secondary teachers were 'invited' to apply for the middle school jobs. When Mo had gone back into teaching she had decided to opt for the middle school sector: it would be relatively congenial to teach French without the pressure of examinations. To her consternation not long after the authority decided that, two years on, it would abolish middle schools and conduct a wholesale re-reorganisation with *every* teacher re-applying for their jobs. Middle school teachers would apply for primary or secondary jobs. Now part-time teachers like Mo would have no choice; they would be expected to fill in gaps wherever these occurred. So she decided to improve her prospects by applying for a *full-time* job in another middle school well before the re-reorganisation. Although her new Headmistress made her life a misery she comforted herself with the knowledge that two years down the line she would be moving on. When re-reorganisation – or should that actually be de-reorganisation? – finally came she opted for primary teaching. To her utter dismay she learned that her present school was to be reclassified as a primary and she would be staying put! Together we composed a cunningly crafted letter to the authority giving reasons for wanting to move whilst at the same time appearing supportive of the Head, whose approval would be needed. Mo got her redeployment, with the Head's blessing, to a primary school in the west of the city. She loved it.

As for me, I'd found my feet professionally. Having published a couple of books and a number of academic articles I was promoted to Senior Lecturer. I had also been appointed as Chief Examiner for A Level Politics at the Oxford Board and I enjoyed that responsibility. Whilst at The Briars, in addition to researching politics and literature I had returned to my first area of interest, British political parties. A couple of years before we moved, senior figures in the Labour party, disillusioned with its apparent leftward lurch, had formed a breakaway party, the Social Democrats. Twenty seven other Labour MPs and one Tory joined the new party, which fought the general election of 1983, the year we went to The Briars, in an electoral pact with the Liberals, called The Alliance. British politics would never be the same. Although Labour polled only two percent more than The Alliance it won nearly 200 more seats. British politics, it seemed, would remain pretty much the same after all. I had begun my spell in The Briars with hopes for real political change but Thatcher was still in office – if only just – when I came to leave eight years later. All my adult life I'd hoped for a broad left-of-centre government, and had written about that possibility. Personally and professionally I despaired. It was now as far away as ever.

As the Eighties wore on, Hull University, like the country at large and most of its institutions, fell on hard times. The Vice

Chancellor was convinced that stringent financial cuts were needed, and since staff salaries were by far the largest item in the budget, this would mean shedding staff and maybe closing some departments. Everyone began to look over their shoulder: who was going to be for the chop?

Ch.13: *Cometh the Hour*

President Truman decided that he would appoint only one-armed academic economists as his advisers: other academics are too prone to on-the-one-hand-this-but-on-the-other-hand-that. So although planning can be a good idea, sometimes a very good idea, the idea of academic planning is a bit oxymoronic. That's why Universities have always employed professionals to help them plan – accountants as Finance Officers for example – but many senior administrators came from an academic background. That's why there was usually broad agreement between academics and administrators about what a university was *for*, though they may have disagreed about how to run their institution. In my many dealings with other institutions I was struck by how many academics thought *their own* university was a byword for incompetence. There was a time when this didn't much matter.

Almost unnoticed, though, like good old Topsy, universities had just growed, becoming in the process a significant cost to the public purse. Their traditional inefficiencies were now more apparent as they were teaching a far wider range of ability with no greater resources. Reforms were needed but those that emerged during the Thatcher years proved largely inappropriate: funding was cut, students became 'customers', and administrators rebranded themselves as 'managers' and began to speak a cult language built around concepts like 'robustness' and 'fitness for purpose' and 'front loading' and 'zero-based planning', which meant many things and all of them nasty. The new 'values' that these phrases encapsulated were wrapped up in 'mission statements' showing that universities were 'fit for purpose' (it was no longer assumed that universities knew instinctively what they were about) and this new style of management was embodied in a new medium that *was* its message: powerpoint presentations. Powerpoint exploded the traditional academic/administrator relationship and replaced it with hard-nosed balance-sheet logic. Resistance was mown down in a hail of bullet points.

At Hull the Vice Chancellor, a former academic who certainly didn't fit the picture of administrative incompetence, told a stunned meeting of Senate that the University would need to lose over 100 members of staff to balance its books. Such exercises, the unstated argument ran in government circles, will surely weed out these 'fashionable' areas, like Politics or Sociology or American Studies? Trouble was, these were the very subjects that drew in the punters and hence the funding and they were also the cheapest subjects to teach. So when costs were cut it was precisely the kind of hard-edged subject that the government would have liked to protect like applied sciences that tended to suffer.

Many Vice Chancellors came up with the same devious scheme: get Heads of Department or Deans of Faculty to prepare plans for their own Departments and Faculties, identifying strengths, and by extension weaknesses and showing how these could be built up – or cut down. That made these VCs look democratic and, even better, meant someone else took the tough decisions. Throughout the land, Heads and Deans called colleagues together to devise such plans. This was like telling people that you intend to gas some of them and then asking each for 50p for the meter, or so I and my colleagues argued when Wilfred Potts called a meeting to devise such a plan for Politics. Potts was unmoved: 'You should be more confident in your achievements,' he told us: 'this Department doesn't have any weaknesses.' He would draw up a plan and then we would see. When it arrived, the plan proved not to have managed the impossible after all – quite the opposite: in highlighting areas of strength it exposed areas and individuals who hadn't been highlighted. But of course they *had* been highlighted – as expendable. The subsequent departmental meeting was explosive and Potts closed it after ten minutes or so, accepting that his plan had no support. A few days later word came that Potts had tendered his resignation and it had been accepted. The man had had his fill of poisoned chalices. Immediately an election for the next Head of Department was organised and I was chosen. A part of me was exhilarated since I would be the first ever elected Head of Politics at Hull but the larger part of me was stunned both by a realisation of my new administrative responsibilities – I was there because my colleagues trusted me – and by the knowledge that I would have to face exactly the same problems that had born Potts down. I wasn't overawed; after all, I was no whizz-kid. Now in my forties I had chaired the Senate's Schools Liaison Committee and was subsequently invited to sit on other committees, chairing some, and so about the time the financial problems at the University came to a head, what with running a hall of residence as well, I had become the most experienced administrator in the Department after Potts.

Some weeks after my appointment I went to my first Faculty Planning meeting and the Dean proposed that centrally imposed staff cuts be shared among departments *pro rata*. Politics would lose two members of staff. He sought the approval of each Head of Department and each in turn reluctantly agreed. I was the sixth of seven to be asked. I argued that this was an un-plan and that the Faculty Planning Committee should live up to its name and produce a *real* plan, one that identified strengths, showing how the Faculty meant to protect them, and weaknesses too, allowing these to atrophy. The last Head to speak, though he represented one of the weaker, and larger departments, supported me. The Dean put his proposal to the vote and it was carried by five to two. At the end of the meeting I stated that I was going to pursue my argument 'elsewhere'. The Dean exploded: this was a direct challenge. Courageous, independent stance? Well, wasn't I proposing for the Faculty *exactly* what Potts had tried for the Department? The way I saw it, I was trying to defend the Department first against Potts and then against the Dean. So: hypocritical or consistent? To be honest, I still don't know. Anyway, my argument was ignored, just as Potts' had been. But I did go to see the VC.

How do you identify someone for early retirement or 'voluntary' redundancy? Normally age, area of expertise and publications record. Politics had one sixty-year old with a short list of publications. Cultured, charming and well-informed, in the prevailing climate his position was not easily defended. The next day I went to see him, told him that we wanted him in the Department, that he could be certain I would fight hard to keep him, but he should realistically assume that he was going to be pressured into leaving. His eyes closed, his whole frame sagged and shuddered involuntarily: I watched as his career and self-esteem imploded before me. This was not what I had come into the academic world to do and there and then I decided that I would resist being sucked deeper into the quagmire of university administration. Why help to lead an institution in what, as far as I was concerned anyway, was exactly the wrong direction?

I lost that fight, though Wilfred Potts, like a knight in shining armour, found our man a job overseas. In fact he thrived after leaving Hull. On the other hand Politics lost no other member of staff, so I won a small victory. Surprisingly the Administration managed to persuade a sufficient number of staff to leave to balance its books, but it would be nonsense to believe that this left the University on the whole leaner and fitter. One academic refused and became the first in Britain to be made compulsorily redundant, and he and the union took the case all the way to the House of Lords. The University won finally in 1992.

This cost-cutting exercise turned out to be only part of the agenda of radical reform; more followed. First came the Research Assessment Exercise in which all departmental heads had to submit a detailed account of their colleagues' research activities, which would be graded nationally and funding would follow the grading. How could the *quality* of research, in the Arts and Humanities at any rate, be measured? Forget Donald Rumsfeld's unknown unknowns; this is an unknowable unknown. The only thing that might realistically be measured in the short term is quantity and that's what was measured: publication for its own sake became a professional duty. As it happened Politics at Hull came out well but the exercise on the whole was self-defeating and sometimes damaging in its consequences.

Now to reform teaching! Every department in the land was to be assessed and graded for the quality of its teaching. Again financial support would follow the grading. The procedure required a vast amount of paperwork and many weeks of valuable time both for assessors and assessed. A report on the work of every department in the country would be available in all school and public libraries to inform the choice of every prospective student – every 'stakeholder'. At a large conference of Politics teachers after the results were published I discovered that few of them and even fewer of their students had made or intended to make any effort to consult these reports. As an assessment team leader I saw the whole process from all angles. A professional inspectorate has plusses and minuses: this system, I concluded, only has minuses.

But the quest for economy and efficiency didn't end here: now universities were 'encouraged' to restructure themselves. Traditionally British universities comprised generic institutions known as Faculties: Arts and Humanities, Life Sciences, Engineering and so on, and these comprised a number of individual Departments. It was the Faculties' formal responsibility to monitor what Departments taught, how they taught it, how they examined it, how they managed discipline and so on. Faculties might influence or even control departmental appointments. Faculty Deans ran large, complex offices and were paid an honorarium. Heads of Department were paid a lesser honorarium for managing smaller offices. No doubt there was some overlap and inefficiency but there was also an Oakshottian synergy about the relationship: we knew how to make it work. Now Faculties and Departments were to be swept away and replaced by intermediate units, Schools. There were so many obvious pitfalls to this massively time-consuming exercise at the practical level that it should never have gone ahead. It further deflected academics from doing what they were supposed to do, *what they were now being measured and graded for doing.* In due course fourteen Schools emerged at Hull and though they were reasonably coherent nearly all encompassed disabling animosities and unseemly internal struggles for resources. Within five years the system had collapsed and Hull was back to Faculties and Departments, though by this time I had escaped. Impossible to quantify just how much time and effort was wasted on these exercises or how morale-sapping each was.

For myself, running the Department, preparing for the first research and teaching assessments, fighting the Department's corner in the restructuring debacle and looking after the Hall made me a busy man, especially given my responsibilities as an A Level Chief Examiner. My workload was increased even more when I was asked to chair the new Board of Undergraduate Studies, which tried to do the work of the old Faculty Boards, and its antennae stretched everywhere. I learned a lot about how the University was administered; discovering for example that for the previous three years some students had been graduating on a degree that didn't formally exist. I chose not to tell anyone! I noted some of the absurd disparities between School marking standards. I took no consolation from the knowledge that after reorganisation things were getting worse.

All this administrative experience strengthened my hand should I wish to apply for a Chair in another university. And why not? For family reasons I hadn't considered leaving Hull before but by this time the boys had flown the nest: Tim had followed Josh, going up to Huddersfield to study Architecture. Kathleen hadn't yet reached the age where moving would present a major problem. In 1988 I had been invited for interview for a Chair in Auckland, which, even by air, turned out to be as far away as ever.

The country was a revelation. Gone was the stolid, grainy egalitarianism. Now those with money splashed it around and those without, often urban Maori, tried to wrest some from those who had it. Drugs and alcoholism were rife in parts of the major cities and in addition those cities had more of a Polynesian feel. The country was livelier, brighter, more welcoming and more dangerous. How many town centre guest houses would leave the key in their front doors at night now? I was offered the post but decided, after discussions with Mo and the children on my return, to turn it down.

All the same we felt it was time for a change. Though I'd come actually to enjoy life at The Briars and relish my relationship with the students, Auckland had given me itchy feet. There were no job prospects in the offing, so we'd have to move back to The Avenues for our change. We began to look for a house at our leisure but to our surprise, we saw exactly what we wanted almost immediately, a delightful Victorian terraced house. We visited twice and decided to make an offer, which was immediately accepted. By the beginning of that December we were the proud owners of the house: now we would be moving at Easter and not summer. Then suddenly, quite out of the blue, something else popped up.

Before we left The Briars I found out from a friend who worked there about a new Chair at the University of Stirling. We had got to know each other when representing our respective universities on recruitment tours of British schools on the continent. Mo, Kathleen and I had visited the McLeans in their large Bridge of Allan home and John and Anisha had visited us in Hull. So when the University of Stirling proposed to reinstate its Politics Department – formally closed but stubbornly refusing to die –

with the appointment of a Chair, it was natural that John should mention it to his friend. It was equally natural that the prospect of helping to build up a Department – though it would never be as big as Hull's – rather than managing the decline of one would appeal to said friend. What's more, with my focus on building up a small Department I would not be expected to involve myself in more senior administration. I could find time for my own research.

On a sunny day in late February I was interviewed. Things could have gone better and I came away convinced that I had missed out. As my train glided down the East Coast in the late afternoon, looking back towards the north I saw Lindisfarne Castle silhouetted against the winter sky: behind it a stream of gold and orange spilled out along the horizon over a remarkably placid North Sea. Suddenly the world didn't seem such a bad place. OK I might have failed to get the job, but having missed out on dinner the day before I had earned the right to a good meal on the University this evening. Gin and tonic in my hand, I ordered Thai fishcakes for starters and venison for the main course and sat back to take in this remarkable end to a winter's day. After an excellent meal followed by cheese, coffee and brandy, I felt able to contemplate my likely failure with something close to equanimity. Arriving home at about 9.30pm I was greeted by surprising news: the Principal at Stirling had phoned and would be phoning again shortly. When the call came I was offered the job and given two days to reach a decision. 'Congratulations,' said Mo when I told her, managing an unconvincing smile. Just now, enjoying her teaching more than ever, a move to Scotland was the last thing she wanted. Kathleen, who had stayed up to hear the news, rushed upstairs crying. I took the bottle of champagne that had been put in the fridge the day before 'just in case' and replaced in quietly in the wine rack.

We talked things over at considerable length the next evening and decided that I should take the job. That night I wrote a brief letter to my dad. He had always complained of being the last person in the family to be told things. This time he would be the first. His son, who had been deprived of the *Beano* because he was too lazy to pass the Eleven Plus, was about to become a Professor – in Scotland, a part of these islands he had always loved. To be honest I have always believed that Marx's maxim – Groucho's not Karl's – was spot on: he wouldn't wish to patronise any club willing to have him as a member. If I achieved anything, like this promotion, the fact that *I* had achieved it lessened its value. But I knew what pleasure and pride my parents would take from this news; it meant that I had repaid them a bit.

One of the other natural but far from pleasant features of reaching a professorial age is the exposure to general mortality. Some among the older generation in our families began to shuffle off their mortal coils, two of Mo's uncles departing the world in our years at The Briars. On my side my Aunt Alice, so much part of my childhood and youth, had died of cancer only a year after our return from New Zealand. It had been my first experience of that painful emptiness that comes with the death of someone near. Alice probably had always shown a more instinctive understanding of and sympathy for me than my mother had. Her husband Paul had been beside himself with grief.

My mum and dad on the other hand seemed to be in rude health. On my dad's seventieth birthday when they came up to Hull I arranged for us to go up to the very top of the Humber

Bridge, then nearing completion, with one of the engineers, and walk down one of the huge suspension cables, with its wire mesh walkway and handrails. I thought that would be a memorable experience for him and so it turned out to be: scared the life out of him, he said later. Then one morning about four years later, I got a call from James: our indestructible dad had had a mild stroke. A complete recovery was expected but I found his sudden vulnerability very upsetting. As I had grown up my dad and I were often at loggerheads. In many things, most of them unimportant, I knew more than he did and didn't miss the opportunity to make him aware of this. For example, he despised drugs and drug users and when I told him in my superior way that alcohol and nicotine were about the most dangerous of drugs he did his pieces. How could I possibly say these were *drugs*? I very much regret now that I didn't deploy my knowledge more sensitively. All the same I became very close to him later, especially after I had become a father myself. The thought that he was destructible after all was undermining.

In the autumn of 1990 my parents and James and Nicky came up for a long weekend. Both my parents were as brown as berries but when we three men went for a walk on the Sunday morning, my dad returned to the Hall after only ten minutes claiming to be tired. James and I were surprised but not alarmed. As winter approached however the family became increasingly concerned. My dad was clearly not well. His tan had given way to an unhealthy pallor; he had no energy and was losing weight. In February of 1991 he was diagnosed with oesophageal cancer, and as it developed through the spring he declined alarmingly. He was having to expectorate almost constantly and carried a bowl around the house. We visited several times and always he tried to put up a show. Fortunately for me life was very full at that time but at quiet moments I would feel my despair as a sharp physical pain. I had always found security in my dad's great strength. Now this Celtic warrior was like a wraith shuffling around the house dragging his spittoon; eyes that had burned bright throughout my life had suddenly grown dim.

It was fortunate that my attention was mainly absorbed by organising our departure. Though convinced that we were doing the right thing, in many ways we were sorry to be leaving The Briars and were touched by the huge 'thank you' card signed by so many of the inmates and the chunky Edinburgh crystal brandy goblets we received as a parting gift. Both boys were home and able to help with our move when it came and in no time at all we had established ourselves in our new home. No walls to dismantle this time, no Hull matches to miss! By now we had a deep attachment to the city and to the East Riding. We had come to Hull expecting to stay two or three years, not twenty-three years. Mo and Kathleen would spend two more years before moving north and for me there would be two years of commuting, but from the summer of 1991 we knew that our future was to lie in Scotland. The colleague who was saddest to see me go was Robert Nagy. I would miss his wisdom and his friendship, but otherwise I was excited by the prospect of a new challenge.

Ch.14: *The Lure of the North*

Just after midnight Woggle the cat did a massive pee in the back of the car, imparting a fragrance that would stay with us for months. Welcome to Scotland! But who could blame him? He'd been cooped up in his little travel kennel for five hours on the journey from Hull to Stirling and had been as good as gold. Moving is one of the greatest strains on married life. Our move to Scotland, our ninth, was, until then anyway, what the French might call a *tranche de gateau*. A house key was supposed to have been waiting for us at the porter's lodge at the University but when we arrived just after midnight there was no key. It was at that point that Woggle's resolve deserted him.

Woggle and his friend Zorba had been replacements for the late lamented Winkle. They had come as a job lot from an acquaintance in The Avenues and then accompanied us to The Briars. Zorba was a bold and muscular beast of limited intelligence who was always blamed when damage was done. He *looked* like a criminal. It was only when his untimely death led to no diminution whatever in the crime rate that the history of this pair was reappraised. Woggle, the smiling villain, had returned to The Avenues in 1990. Now he was going to chance his arm in Scotland.

So, what had happened to the key whose absence did for Woggle's bladder? We'd had to leave Hull some time after the removers, because after Pickfords had emptied it, we needed to get the house ready for new occupants – it was to be rented out. It was early evening before we left Hull. Our friends the McLeans, who were on holiday at the time, had offered their house for the night and John's secretary Jean was to leave the key – *the* key – with the University porter. It was nearly 12.30am when, after a cursory exploration of her office, the University porter found no key. He hadn't the secretary's number on file, and though I knew her name there turned out to be an unreasonable number of McIntoshs and Macintoshs in the area. Fortunately my own secretary was a friend of Jean: she would know her number. So at 12.45am I phoned Betty. Jemmied out of her sleep Betty came up with Jean's number and shortly before 1am I roused an irate man who knew nobody called Jean McIntosh – or Macintosh – and wasn't too thrilled to be asked. Had Betty got the number wrong or had I misdialled? Only one way to find out! My man stuck to his story, rather ferociously actually. Back again to Betty, who came up with a different number this time. At 1.20am a man at the end of the new number confessed to the name of Macintosh. 'Jean, there's some guy here who seems to know you and he's going on about some bloody key.' From the depths came a strangulated cry: 'Oh, my God!' Finally the key was located.

Things could only get better, couldn't they? We got to bed just after 3am, and awoke not ever so much later to a hazy late August sun. The solicitor turned up with the house keys at 9.30am as agreed, we opened the door to our new life and minutes later Pickfords arrived. Everything was offloaded by lunchtime and when we sat down to our evening meal much of the initial hard work had been done.

I'd had a good few heart-to-hearts with Kathleen over the previous weeks, explaining why we were uprooting her and how she had to grit her teeth and tough things out for a week or two;

after all, she was Yorkshire. If she surrendered to her natural misgivings she would only make her mum's life miserable too. The next day was her first at the local High School and off she went stoically. When she came home Kathleen ran straight upstairs, chucked stoicism out the window and cried her eyes out. This was the first day of the rest of her life! Next morning she had a stomach ache and couldn't possibly go to school. She had to be strong, we said, and she had to go: off she went in dudgeon. At 4pm she charged in, much like the day before and rushed upstairs. Down almost immediately she asked if we could have dinner early that evening as she'd been invited out by some new friends.

She had transferred in time to start her Standard Grade courses and went on to do well, finishing up two years later with eight 'A's and a 'B'. The following year her performance in Highers was just as good, and she won the History Prize, so she found herself qualified to fulfil her dream as a four-year old and enter any Scottish university to study law: she chose Strathclyde. She had no trouble, after graduating, in getting a placement, a traineeship and finally a job. When asked later about her schooling in Hull and Dunblane she would always say that what struck her most was that the classes in Dunblane were quiet and amazingly, by and large, the students did what they were told.

Mo's career in Scotland turned out to be less successful. Having been accepted for voluntary redundancy she had left Hull with a small income but she was keen to take up teaching again. She had little trouble in gaining the necessary official recognition. Her move north couldn't have been better timed, it seemed. Scotland had just begun a programme to encourage all primary children to learn French. Not only would any primary school jump at taking her on but with her experience she might reasonably expect some advisory position in the programme of instruction leading to the certificate for these would-be teachers of French. So we were reliably told. In fact she wasn't even allowed to teach French in Scotland *at all* because she didn't have the new one-year certificate for beginners! The fact that she had studied French to degree level and taught French at each level to university entrance counted for *nothing*. Nor was her advice ever sought in delivering the certificate programme. So she remained a supply teacher, teaching just about everything except French, and encountering anti-English prejudice from time to time amongst pupils and staff. On the other hand she had some super classes and she especially enjoyed two long-term placements at Catholic schools in Falkirk where she could hardly have been happier. When finally she decided to hang up her biro she became involved in voluntary work, placing senior citizens in primary schools where they might use their experience and expertise in some aspect of the teaching programme. Mo proved a very competent administrator. So the move north turned out to be a success after all.

As for me, helping to build up even a small university department was an exciting business. I found my three new colleagues, each very different, a pleasure to work with. Battle-hardened in the struggle to keep the department going through several bleak years, they were very willing to make the most of the opportunity to grow. Anticipating Labour's commitment when next in government to set up a Scottish parliament, we appointed an expert in Scottish politics. We also made appointments in European Politics and International Politics and

Political Thought. We became eight: four men, four women; four Brits, two Americans, a German and a French woman.

Teaching Politics at Stirling was rewarding. There were no hatchet men, or women, as there had been at Hull, no 'robust' agenda for reform. I became immersed in my research, attending more overseas conferences than before, reading and writing more. These were by far the best years of my professional life and I was as happy as a sandboy. My research led to the publication of several books and articles. The burgeoning young Department contained some delightful men and women, was a happy and productive outfit and was well thought of. However, as I was about to retire as its Head in 2002, a new University Principal, instead of providing the additional resources that successive review bodies had strongly and consistently recommended, cut the departmental budget and my successor was obliged to manage a deteriorating situation. Not at all the kind of legacy I had wished my friend to inherit, though in the event he managed it astutely.

Just about all Scottish degree courses last for four years, the first being broader in range than most courses elsewhere in the UK. Students tend to have a wider vision, which I think is a great advantage. Their commitment to the discipline is probably weaker, their commitment to learning probably stronger. I found them less enquiring than their English counterparts but a pleasure to teach. I was nonplussed by the sectarian animosities that regularly manifested themselves on toilet walls and occasionally in patterns of behaviour. I had never before experienced problems from students who had enjoyed a liquid lunch, but I did in Stirling. After one post-prandial lecture I tried to collar a guy who kept whispering penetrating observations to a colleague throughout my lecture. He shot off before I could speak to him so I wrote, told him very forcefully that this behaviour was unacceptable and to see me the next day. In he subsequently came, looking very agitated and I was ready for a confrontation. He threw the letter on the table: 'Professor Spring, how can I apologise? That you should have to write to me to complain of me behaving like a schoolboy! I am so ashamed. What would my mother say?' There is so much about the Scots that I admire.

My feeling of general well-being was reinforced by the fact that I was working in a place of rugged natural beauty. The campus paraded a panoramic grandeur of rich colour and a spaciousness enhanced by the purple Ochil hills in the immediate background, and by the rugged Trossachs off to the west. On a clear winter's day a necklace of snow-capped peaks would glisten like pearls. On some other days the Wallace Monument and the ramparts of Stirling Castle would pierce the mists that hung over the Carse – an almost mediaeval vision. This was the kind of place you came to on holiday, not the place you lived in. Unless you were very lucky. These Stirling years went by at a gallop.

In the real world of politics though things were not so rosy. In 2003 Blair led Britain, along with the US and the 'coalition of the willing' into an invasion of Iraq – the Second Gulf War – with disastrous long-term consequences. Blair's government, welcomed so rapturously in 1997, came to be despised and a chasm opened up between the people – including at least one Professor of Politics – and their representatives. From around this time I began to lose interest in the practice of politics, especially with the rise of Scottish nationalism. I have never felt at ease with nationalisms.

The Iraq invasion was an indirect consequence of an event that was as dramatic as any since the Cuban Missile Crisis: Nine-Eleven. I was chairing a Departmental 'away-day' meeting when the manager of the hotel came into the room and broke the news: come and see the television, she implored. We had to abandon our meeting. I was due to fly to Helsinki the next day to deliver a paper to a conference. I couldn't do it. What was the point?

At the personal level, meanwhile, Mo and I were transmogrifying into the older generation. The Grim Reaper, who had only made the odd foray into our lives so far, would mark these next years with death. The year after our move north was dominated by my dad's inexorable dying. Commuting between Hull and Stirling, I managed to get down to see him from time to time from Hull. He had been operated on in the early summer and the doctors had pronounced the operation a success. He was sent home and told to walk after a few days. Just a hundred yards at first, building up gradually day by day. On one visit shortly after, I accompanied him and it was obvious that he was getting weaker, not stronger. But this was my dad and he kept extending his walks as instructed. Our walk on that day took us to the local library where, to my surprise, my first book was on the shelves. My dad took it out and showed it to the librarian. 'See this?,' he said, and pointed to me, 'it's my son here wrote it.' My achievements, insignificant in the great scheme of things, meant so much to them. This book had been a kind of vindication of all the sacrifices they had made on my behalf through the years. For me this was the best of moments and it was the worst of moments. As I left that evening I said goodbye to my dad for the last time.

One afternoon about a month later I was called to the telephone: it was James – our dad was on the point of death. 'Don't rush down, mate,' he said, 'according to the doc he's only got a few hours.' I had come up by car that week and given the lack of urgency, it made sense to drive back to Hull and catch the usual train down to London the next morning. When I arrived in Hull I phoned again: he was hanging on but couldn't survive the night. I planned to take the usual train which would get me to No.12 at 12.25pm. Before leaving I phoned again: he had survived the night but death was imminent. I drove to the station and for the one and only time in twenty-five years I found myself in a traffic jam, missed my train and had to take the equivalent, an hour later, arriving at 1.25pm. My cousin Kevin came out to meet me and to tell me that my dad had died about 12.40pm. Nothing could persuade me, then or now, that he hadn't been waiting for me and that, as so often when I was younger, I had let him down. He was eighty-two.

All the extended family managed to get to the funeral and he had just the send off he would have wanted. A couple of months later on a suitably pinched November afternoon, my mum, James and I allowed my dad's ashes to drop gently into the Thames where they belonged. He wasn't the only person close to me who died in the September of 1991. At the age of fifty-seven Robert Nagy suffered an aneurysm. I hurried down to see him in hospital but a few days later my good friend died. Just like my dad's, Robert's funeral took place in fine autumn sunshine; they were separated only by a week.

My mum coped very well: she read a lot and watched a lot of sport on TV. She came up to Scotland several times over the years, including for Josh's graduation in Edinburgh. Later she loved the weekly visit from Josh, who was then working in London; they would watch *The Sweeney* together. Only in the last few years did her back lose its straightness. Her lifelong smoking, though she gave up towards the end, left her with increasingly debilitating emphysema and eventually she found it difficult to move. In the summer of 1997 Mo and I visited her for a weekend on our way down for a holiday in France. She complained that she never saw us and that we used No.12 like a hotel. I explained how busy I was: I had been in Oxford for the whole of the previous week and immediately on our return would be flying to Seoul. She seemed to understand. On the Monday morning we packed the car and I popped up for a last minute pee when my back went into spasm: a memento of my rugby days. I spent the next week in a close relationship with a large bag of frozen peas. We stayed at No.12 for five days and Mo did all the shopping and the cooking and we had wine from Asda every day. I heard later from a cousin that my mum had admitted to being secretly glad I'd hurt my back: she got to see more of us than she had for ages. Three months later she was dead.

She had fallen and broken her hip but when recovering in London Hospital had developed a chest infection. I had been to see her when she was still quite chirpy but she deteriorated quickly and I came down again, my journey seriously interrupted by the IRA. My mum was unconscious when I arrived and James and I sat disconsolately at her bed. I began to talk about our childhood and thought, wishfully, that maybe she could hear. But James wanted to discuss practical and financial issues. Well, he had been with her in her last years and I had been 500 miles away; he had the right to call the shots and these things did need to be discussed. But I could have dissuaded him from talking 'business'; I *should* have dissuaded him, but I didn't. When I got back to Dunblane that evening I wept bitterly for my mum but for myself too. I had managed to let down both my parents at the last. Next day my mum died. Somewhere a cock must have crowed. Whatever I may have achieved was principally my mum's doing. Her faith in both her sons' ability to succeed, sorely tested by me in those early years, was the driving force in James' and my life. She had always stood behind me even when neither of us knew where I was going.

This was in 1997, an eventful year in which Kathleen went up to university leaving us on our own for the first time after twenty-seven years. But the previous year had been so much more eventful: on March 13th, the sky had fallen in on our home township of Dunblane when sixteen five-year old primary school children and one of their teachers were shot dead by a disaffected loner. Mo had taught at the school often and indeed had been asked to teach there that very week, but was already committed elsewhere. No words could even come close to describing the numbing effect this act of evil brutality had on our local community. Dunblane was a small essentially decent place where nothing much happened: suddenly it became the centre of the planet, and for the worst of reasons. Mo and I, just like every other citizen of Dunblane, received dozens of calls from friends wanting to be sure we, especially Kathleen, were alright. Seventeen local homes would never be alright. At around 2am two days later Nathan Samuels phoned from Peru where he was on business; he had only just heard.

When I was young I had often wondered whether I would live to see the Millennium: well finally here it was and it turned out to be an anticlimax; how can you calibrate upwards from celebrating a new beginning that happens every twelve months to one that happens every thousand years? On New Year's Day 2000 after a short illness Woggle died, aged about 20: he at least showed a sense of occasion. We entered the new Millennium feeling blessed. Kath was maturing into a delightful and very able young woman. Josh had taken a job in London where he had put his considerable analytical skills to good use. He had a steady girl friend and they had set off on a world tour a month or so before the millennium. On their return they would marry and set up home in Edinburgh. Having graduated in Architecture with a poor degree caused largely by ill-health, Tim's subsequent plans to make money through design work proved to be impractical and he became unemployed: he was very low. I had a thought: Nathan was running a small frame-making business in Dewsbury and might have a labouring job for Tim. Yes, as luck would have it, he did! So at last Tim was earning. He pulled his weight, got on with his mates who were a pretty tough lot and grew visibly in self-confidence. He applied for and got funding for an EU evening course on Computer Aided Design and flourished. To cap it all he was allowed to repeat the final year of his undergraduate degree and improve his degree classification. He subsequently went off to Leeds to do postgraduate work. Jobs in Leeds and London followed.

And all this time Doreen had just been chugging along, getting a bit smaller and a bit frailer each year. She was showing herself less able to manage in that Spartan house, and we were so far away. Fortunately a local 'old boy' would come in and light her fire, do her shopping and keep an eye on her. Eventually though frozen pipes drove her into a residential home, temporarily at first but then permanently. She was comfortable, got lots of visitors and was very well cared for. She never came north now but we got down to see her reasonably often: Mo would travel down by train; the lads, especially Tim, took the trouble to drive down – or up. Josh and his wife took her great-grandson down to see her. On Easter Sunday 2005 she died of pneumonia aged 95. At last she would be rejoining Henry. Doreen's last words were in reply to the offer of an orange juice: 'Couldn't put a drop of gin in it could you?'

What is it Hamlet's uncle tells him? The death of parents though a cause of sorrow – even when not brought on by a phial of poison rammed up the ear – is an inevitable part of life. But death is not our only companion in later years: Josh and his wife produced their son in 2003: a daughter would follow later. Other good things happened: Tim had found himself a partner whom we took to immediately and whom he would marry later. Kathleen began to enjoy real success in her legal career and moved down to London. She and her partner would eventually produce a fine son.

Meanwhile the new Millennium had risen gingerly to its feet, shaken itself down and begun its forward march. My retirement was now in prospect, that dry run for Sinatra's final curtain, Bach's *der alte Bund.* But for Mo and me the best part of the day had always been the evening; it was around this time in our lives that we began to travel abroad again – lots – suggesting that these years might be as good as any. After all, the sun's over life's yardarm where we are: Gin and Tonic? We wouldn't mind if we did.

Ch.15: *Time's Chariot*

It's easy to die if the things you care about are going to survive... that's how people used to see it. Individually they were finished, but their way of life would continue. Their good and evil would remain good and evil.

(George Orwell, *Coming Up for Air*.)

Some thinkers tell us a life only finally makes sense with death. Sophocles reckoned that no one could be judged happy, for example, until they actually carried that happiness down to the grave. I'm still around and who knows what the fates have in mind? I think as you get older you should live as if you'll be around forever whilst knowing you might pop your clogs tomorrow, or succumb to the privations promised by Jacques in *As You Don't Like It*. So: I'm taking stock now.

I grew up in a world in which though most people weren't really religious, Christianity shaped the public consciousness. We were decent people: I knew there was right and wrong and which was which, and I knew wrong would be punished. I had a strict moral upbringing: my mum always ironed my underpants. (Blessed are those whose underpants are ironed, it says in the *Apocrypha* – approximately – for the gates of the city will be open to them.) One lunchtime, when I was coming home from Primary School on the bus – I would have been nine or ten – a girl was playfully pinching me and pulling my hair. I was trying to push

June away when, as we approached our stop, the driver applied the brakes sharply. My casual push became a hand-off that any rugby winger would have been proud of. As we got off I told her to stop crying: it had been her own fault. My dad was at home that lunchtime and we'd hardly started lunch when there was a knock at the front door. June and her dad stood on the doorstep and a rather partisan account of events was given. My dad asked for my explanation, which I admit sounded thin. There and then I was given three whacks of the cane, with June's dad pleading for leniency. I'd broken the code. Yes, we were decent people.

Children weren't sent up chimneys any more, it's true, but they knew their place and by and large they did what they were told. Most people got married in church, almost nobody got divorced, their children were baptised in church and they had church funerals when they died – and nobody left this world to the strains of *I'm Forever Blowing Bubbles*. After a death in the family women wore black and even men would wear a black armband. And Sunday was a day of rest. Fair enough, as we grew up most of my generation wanted to shake up this torpidity, but we emphatically did *not* want the pattern of life disintegrating into a kaleidoscope of moral relativism. We wouldn't even have known what that was if it had pulled us by the todger.

With the decline in the Church's influence the structure of morality that it championed began to lose its shape. Homosexuality, for example, was both a sin and a crime. Now it is neither. Good job too, most people would say. I grew up believing that the state was morally justified in taking the life of anyone who committed a murder. Now even the Pope says that's immoral. When a church leader like David Jenkins, one-time Bishop of Durham, declared that he didn't believe in the

Resurrection, you knew the game was up. (But did he *really* think he was the first? Anyway, shortly after his consecration at York the Minster was struck by lightning!) Even marriage is now an optional extra and a commitment for life is becoming a thing of the past. Perhaps people live too long these days. In the traditional marriage the man was dominant. Modern Britain is no paradigm of gender equality but huge changes have taken place in the relationship between men and women.

My childhood had been monochrome but amazingly in my teenage years our world suddenly became Technicolour – and then pixelated. Large-scale immigration from the West Indies and then the Indian subcontinent ensured that Britain's cities really did become Technicolour. But the origin and emblem of wider change was rock-and-roll, which turned out to be the herald of a full-blown social revolution. I and most of my mates were originally just as enthusiastic about this revolution as William Wordsworth had been about the French Revolution. When asked, in *The Wild One*, what he was rebelling against, Marlon Brando spoke for a generation of rebels without a cause when he replied: 'What've you got?' Yet by the 1980s these changes, later to be inflated by the technological revolution, were sweeping onwards, leaving me and others behind. How could we have known that in the shadow of Bill Haley lurked a host of Johnny Stinkers, Burt Cocaines and nihilistic Oi Boys? This really was a new class, revolutionary and fairly equal, but hardly the soberly socialist one George Orwell had envisaged. The eclipse of the cultural old guard and the decline of institutional religion in Britain hasn't so far led to a collapse in public morality – quite the opposite in some areas, such as support for charities and 'good works'. What's more that decline led to the exposure of a frightening array of abuses of power on the part of some of those religious institutions, leading many to conclude that we're better off without them. Nevertheless society today is not the same, as the seismic shifts in *The Archers* plot lines show: an everyday story of moral collapse!

Just as British society has changed dramatically during my life, so has its politics, and for me, a student of politics who once had political ambitions, these changes have been particularly significant. In the Britain of my youth the great majority of people were staunch supporters of one or other of the two main parties, according, mainly, to their class, and few people changed their allegiance. With the decline of large-scale manufacture, traditional socialism began to lose its way just at the time when those institutions that held the old Tory party together – church, empire, monarchy and family – were in eclipse. This allowed Margaret Thatcher's brand of hard-nosed Conservatism to dominate the ideological landscape and destroy what she and her friends dismissed as the cosy post-war consensus – 'decency' as I would have called it.

For me *the* pivotal political event of the period occurred in 1984: the National Union of Mineworkers went on an unballoted national strike. I had watched the urban race riots of the early 1980s in disbelief, though I scarcely knew the areas concerned. Now my own country was being destroyed, not so much by rioters as by the forces of the Snow Queen. One Sunday evening in high summer, after a weekend up at The Longhouse, the family drove back across the county and at one point we were obliged to crawl slowly through a normally empty village. Unmarked white vans were parked everywhere around a green crawling with clean-cut young men calling out in London accents. The police. The next day was Monday June 18th: the Battle of Orgreave. Northern working-class communities were being ripped apart and a way of life was about to be consigned to history along with most mines, steel and textile mills, factories, docks and deep-sea fishing fleets.

Tony Blair, who became leader of the Labour party ten years later, had seen the withering away of Labour's support base in Britain and the even more dramatic dissolution of international socialism, or at any rate the Soviet version of it. He cut Labour adrift from socialism. Without it Labour won the next election at a canter. Four years later, in 2001, the party had more millionaires than miners in its new intake. Socialism and egalitarianism were carefully excised from the party rhetoric. Blair put the kibosh finally on my own already dwindling political certainties.

But the two-party system was already broken. In a growing number of areas – like energy, food, the environment, infrastructure, health provision and defence – policy required a long-term perspective. Yet the rationale of two-party politics demands exactly the opposite. Anyway, I'd closely observed a two-party democracy at work in the New Zealand education system and it had given me the heebie-jeebies. The voice of the people, they say, is the voice of God: but wasn't it 'the people' who chose Barabbas over Christ? Ibsen's 'enemy of the people' said majorities were always wrong and minorities always right. I wouldn't go that far but I'm really wary of the so-called wisdom of the crowd. It was this wisdom, after all, that, when invited to name Britain's new polar exploration vessel overwhelmingly chose Boaty McBoatface. Bernard Shaw said ruling was a skill, like dentistry. Well, who'd want their neighbours making decisions affecting their dental health? (Actually I wouldn't mind: we live next door to a dental practice.) Now and again we probably all think that the government should follow Brecht's advice: dissolve the people and choose another lot. My New Zealand research pointed me towards the notion of balance in a political system. Paradoxically partisan party politics are acceptable as an instrument of modern government only when they don't really work, as in Britain's post-war consensus years. Until recently US politics were in reality non-partisan. Nowadays partisanship is rampant, hugely time-consuming, massively expensive and utterly dysfunctional. Have I said enough?

As I grew up, I sort of assumed that I would be involved in helping to change society through the political process – from a left-wing perspective. It came as a shock to discover that most ordinary people didn't actually want society changed; they just wanted to be better off. Social equality? That's for the birds. Now I've watched birds in southern Africa called sociable weaver birds. They nest in massive trees and invite other sociable weaver birds to join them. In fact any community-minded bird or indeed any sociable flying insect is welcome, though the latter's contribution is likely to be of a dietary nature. So many join these arboreal utopias, building their own nests that the combined weight of birds and nests eventually brings the whole tree crashing down. Borne down by social equality! It's not even for the birds.

So mine – ours – was a landscape of social and political change. What did these changes actually amount to? No doubt every generation sees itself fighting a rearguard action on behalf of civilisation against the barbarians but I've a feeling that John Updike was right to suggest that the disappearance of the traditional fear that we might have to account for our actions at a trial on 'the brightest, furthest quasar' represents a degree of change that scientists would call a paradigm shift. I'm proud to be a member of probably the last generation capable of sitting up straight with arms crossed and *keeping quiet*; proud to be included with those who still insist on the family eating dinner together in a civilised manner; proud to be amongst those who didn't want to lose the discipline of queueing or the custom of giving up seats to the elderly on trains. We had no intention of killing off God, just remodelling Him a bit in our own image. Our generation wanted to keep what it knew and improve on it.

George Orwell saw the writing on the wall more than half a century ago. Modern man, he wrote, is too keen to clear away old beliefs, practices and superstitions. He's like a man up a tree happily sawing away the branch he's sitting on. What he doesn't realise is that underneath isn't a bed of roses but a cesspit full of barbed wire. He was writing about a descent into relativism that has only gathered pace since. I first began to think seriously about moral compasses – right and wrong, that sort of thing – when I was a paper boy. In those days, for me, morality seemed to connect at both the public and personal level to notions of Britishness. Yet at the heart of the notion lies Nurse Cavell's paradox: Britishness is not enough. What's missing – compassion springs to mind – comes from our Judaeo-Christian heritage. It doesn't equate with institutional Christianity but it might be difficult to sustain without the Church. After all the Christian myth shaped the European consciousness for almost two thousand years and now it's disappearing faster than the Greenland ice shelf. Our generation certainly didn't want to finish up in a pit of barbed wire, 'atomised' as Houellebecq put it, yet when we came into our inheritance we turned out to be the very ones who sawed away Orwell's branch.

The American author Bill Bryson wrote an account of a tour he made around Britain in the early 1990s in which he incorporated his impressions of the country gleaned over about twenty years of residency. Twenty years later he wrote a sequel. The Britain he originally came to, he wrote, believed in doing the right thing most of the time whether anyone was watching or not. Not anymore! A tragic loss, he feels. And where is this trajectory heading? In my mind's eye is a metaphor for a possible future: Roger, Jack's sadistic lieutenant in *Lord of the Flies*. At the beginning of the novel, when the boys' behaviour is still governed by the traditional values – and Roger was a choirboy – he would whizz pebbles at the 'little 'uns'. Not to hit them of course, because they were small and defenceless, but to frighten them. It gave Roger a thrill. Towards the end of the story Roger throws stones to hit and he keeps by him a stick sharpened at both ends. This gave him an even bigger thrill. I worry that as institutional Christianity, with all its faults, declines, and as the allures of relativism grow, bloated now by virtual and augmented realities, compassion or what Orwell called 'common decency' – the 'British' attitude to life that Bryson admired – will just fade away. Hope I'm wrong.

Personally I found myself with a dodgy moral compass just when, having taken to foreign travel in a big way, I most needed one. As Richard Holloway said, if there is no *ultimate* meaning to life, how do we find *proximate* meanings? Coming from a society that has all but renounced institutionalised Christianity I needed guidance in lands where millions of people believe, with as strong a faith as mediaeval Christians, in a god with the head of an elephant or the possibility of being reincarnated as a cockroach. I encountered civilisations immeasurably older than mine, and value systems that had served other societies for millennia. The world turned out to be more complex and wonderful than I had believed. I felt as those two Jesuits might have felt when, as the story goes, they were taken through the jungle to see the mighty temple of Angkor Wat. Could they ever look on St. Peter's again with the old unshakable confidence? Well, perhaps they could, but for myself I wasn't so sure.

And of course you need a moral compass to make sense not only of the world at large but of your own life. Fate, destiny, God, who can stand against it (or It)? I never could. I never felt that I shaped my own life. Self-help programmes tell us how to achieve whatever we want. I fell at the first hurdle because I could never conjure up the requisite picture of who I wanted to be or what I wanted to do, could never manage a plan for the future. When I took an early retirement package from my University it dawned on me that I was beginning to run out of future anyway.

As a young boy I lived within my imagination, fed by a love of reading. Wasn't my future always pretty obvious? And then when doing my Finals, I baulked at the idea of emptying my bookshelf: for me, I wanted books to furnish my room. What clearer signal did I need? Nevertheless it took half a lifetime for me to realise that I was destined to be a thinker and teacher rather than a doer, and when the penny finally dropped, it was like a revelation, and to be honest, something of a relief. In my late-thirties I was still thinking of applying for direct entry into the Higher Civil Service, still dreaming of being invited to take on a safe parliamentary seat. A good friend, a manager in a multinational construction company, told me that he asked every applicant for a senior position in his company to send in a paragraph of handwriting for analysis: his graphologist was never wrong. Send me a paragraph, he said, and let's see what you're cut out for. So I did. Back came five pages of character analysis. The graphologist assumed I was another job applicant and wrote that my friend wouldn't regret appointing me, although my skills were best deployed in a creative capacity. Plenty more of this, quite flattering most of it. But then the punch line: 'This man lives in the mind, perhaps too much in the mind.' I had been rumbled! Bernard Shaw said that those who *can* do; those who *can't*, teach. Too simplistic really: after all, teaching hardly constitutes failure. But it wasn't the kind of success that Shaw rated or indeed that I myself had striven for. So, a thinker not a doer! To be fair, I did once cross high over the Yellow River on a dodgy Chinese zip wire, which took some 'doing', but all things considered, the graphologist was right: I became just another village Cromwell guiltless of his country's blood. When he set out for the Americas, Christopher Columbus, they say, had no idea where he was going and when he got there hadn't a clue where he was. That seems a good summary of my journey too.

When I started out on my career as a university teacher most of my students were well to the left politically. Teaching was exciting. By the time I finished there were few in my class who believed in equality or progress. 'We don't need no education' sang Pink Floyd in 1979; no 'dark sarcasm in the class rooms'; no 'thought control'. By the time I finished teaching university staff were no longer even teachers, let alone thought-controllers: we were enablers. Academics still had the opportunity, diminishing though it was, to research and write. I always saw it as an obligation to make my research available to ordinary punters;

after all, they'd paid my salary. I tried never to write or speak just for fellow academics. On the other hand I did retain a strong belief in the value of studying politics – though not political 'science' – as part of a general modern education. Towards the end of my career I spent three years supervising the modernisation of the curriculum of a politics department in a former Soviet republic. I believe this to have been worthwhile: the fewer Institutes of Politology in the world the better. I also believe strongly that great writers like those I studied have a lot to say about politics and life in general; the more people who read them the better. OK, I know these things aren't as important as research directed towards medical advances, renewable energy, or responding to climate change, but they do matter a bit and that has been the best I could offer.

One afternoon Tim and I, on our way down to put some pine cladding up in Doreen's kitchen in Fulton, stopped off at a hardware store to buy the timber. A lad of eighteen or so was manning the checkout and when he saw my name on the banker's card, he asked if I hadn't written a particular book on British political parties. When I owned up, the lad said: 'Let me shake your hand, mate: you got me through my A Level Politics.' For some reward comes in Stockholm with the Swedish Academy; for others it's in B&Q at the checkout.

When that worldly-wise essayist Michel de Montaigne tried to calculate what his life amounted to, he came up not with an answer but with a question: 'Que sçay-je?' – What do I know? My own life has been a journey from a world of moral, social and political certainty into a world of ambiguity, scepticism and relativism. I came to much the same conclusion as Montaigne, though unlike

Michel, I didn't retire to my library but continued to live a full family and community life. To say that my life – our lives – was made fuller by our children and then grandchildren would be to understate. Problems? Sure, lots, and yet so many joys. As for the wider family, we were lucky enough to share the company of three of our four parents for many years. I saw my brother James, Nicky and the family regularly if less frequently as we all got older; we kept in close contact. Poor Jimmy suffered serious ill-health in his later years. His memory and especially his limbs came to fail him but never his spirit. He had been a rock for our mum when she was alone. And cousin David, that lad who couldn't draw, became a well-known architect and created beautiful buildings and received an OBE for 'services to'.

William Morris wrote that fellowship is Heaven and the lack of fellowship Hell. We have many good friends especially those from Sheffield. We've watched each other go very different ways and do very different things over the years; have seen each others' children grow, followed their successes and failures, and now their children's children. We watched in despair as Kieran's Kirsty died from cancer after more than thirty years of marriage. But when we get together for a jar and a chat, as we always have and still do, we are just the same as always – apart from our knees. Not sure this is Heaven exactly, but it's pretty good.

Near the beginning of this story I quoted Shakespeare's Richard III and now near the end I turn back to Richard, or to his motto anyway – *loyauté me lie* – I'm bound by loyalty. I have consciously tried to remain true to the values I inherited – to keep the faith – just as my uncle Paul advised me to on that sunny autumn morning when I set out for Sheffield to conquer the world. Like everybody else I've encountered failure on my journey, loneliness and disillusionment. Sadly the intellectual excitement that consumed me in my undergraduate years, and which I kind of assumed would provide a backdrop to my university career, proved to be short lived; a victim of university reform. Only at Stirling, in the second half of my career, was that excitement reignited at least to some extent. Most of the moral certainties with which I began my journey and which shaped my values seem to have collapsed and yet I still feel an obligation to rescue some lessons from my life that I would want to hand on to our children – I still feel the strength of that quotation from Orwell with which this chapter began. Do these lessons constitute a moral compass? Well, maybe a little one – such as you might get in a Junior Commando set.

Let's start with the Big Question: should our kids believe in a God? For that matter, do I believe in a God? Not sure to both, though my own doubts tend to fall away with the *Agnus Dei* from Bach's B Minor Mass. I do however emphatically believe in a strong community life shaped by Judaeo-Christian values. And I'm *certain* that there are more things in this world than are dreamt of in your philosophy, Horatio. Myself, I hold, and would want my kids to hold firm social, ethical and political beliefs, though I've long since realised there's nothing I can do personally to achieve mine, and I've no grounds for supposing things will be different for our kids. All the same I would advise them that though we can't eradicate poverty, solve the planet's chronic water shortage or save the world from either global warming or terrorism, we can make *our* bit of the world better and fairer: we *can* champion decency. As individuals we have choices. We may not be the masters of our fates – I certainly haven't been – but we *are* the captains of our souls. There is a natural confrontation in life between the letter of the law and the spirit of the law. Wherever we encounter it, as we surely will, we should go with the latter. The law is after all an attempt to make explicit an underlying moral system and sometimes it fails. When push comes to shove, sod the law, I would say. There is an equally universal tension between means and ends: stick firmly with the former would be my advice, and don't be beguiled by utopian ends, which even on a good day tend to put humanity above individual human beings.

Things matter and people matter even more than things, and as political and social and perhaps above all technological change accelerate we've *got* to hold on to that. I would tell my kids they're better off listening to Del Boy with his compassionate faith in family, friends, community and a brighter future than to Montaigne and his pessimism; I'd tell them that there *is* such a thing as society. Their worlds can be better places; they can make a difference. And the reverse is true: all that's needed for evil to triumph – anywhere – is for 'the good' just to cultivate their own gardens. So what my moral compass points to is this: we must stand up for our own values, fight our own corners, and if we all did that, well, who knows where it might lead? The crucial thing is: stick to those values but don't expect too much. 'Most of the time now we settle for half and I like it better,' says Arthur Miller's wise lawyer. Fine, I'll tell my kids, he's right. But you'd better be clear which half – because you'll have to fight for it. And they'll have it tougher than we did, our kids, bringing up children in a world of chemically and technologically enhanced realities where children's 'rights' have challenged traditional family relations. All our parents had to worry about was us getting home in one piece after eight pints of Younger's No.3. When all's said and done, though, it'll be worth the effort: as Del himself would have said: you know it makes sense. And a final word of advice for them: be more careful than we were sawing off branches.